The BEAST Within

DESTROYER OF SOULS

BY: DAVID ALLEN LEARY

ARBOR BOOKS, INC.
19 Spear Road, Ste 301
Ramsey, NJ 07446
www.arborbooks.com
info@arborbooks.com

Printed in the United States

The Beast Within: Destroyer of Souls
David Allen Leary

1. Title 2. Author 3. Biography/Self-Help

Library of Congress Control Number: 2006909221

ISBN 10: 0-9790580-0-7
ISBN 13: 978-0-9790580-0-4

The BEAST Within

DESTROYER OF SOULS

The True Story of:
Evil, Death, Destruction,
Divine Intervention and Salvation

20% Of All Sales From This Book, Will Go Towards
The Development Of A New Concept Program
To Treat Meth & Cocaine Addiction.

BY: DAVID ALLEN LEARY

Contents

Acknowledgements

To the ones who took a chance on purchasing this book. Also to the ones who may have gotten a chance to read it through a friend. Much love in peace. Thanks for allowing me to share this unique story of change with the world.

Buy your book and help to change lives! Would you like to do more to help change the lives of many who are hopeless and lost and near death? I come up with a new concept that may stop hardcore addiction in its tracks. Change is needed; these old programs simply aren't doing enough to help. That's why there is usually a waiting list to get into these programs. Fact: most addicts after treatment return to their drug of choice. This program is for hardcore users only who have a sincere desire to change! If you can help financially with this non-profit concept, let's talk! This is an unorthodox approach to fighting these menaces of society. We are at war, make no mistake about it. Call 602-488-1929.

Dewayne, Fredrick, Leo, Mike Wiley. Thank you for your continued support, I haven't forgotten you. You all know that these have been some very trying times for all of us. It was said before, there's nothing like losing a mother. Thanks to you all from the heart. You are a godsend.

To Amelia Leary. My wife, you and the kids are no doubt a genuine blessing from God. You looked beyond all of my faults and saw my needs. You helped to make me the man I am today. Your heart is pure, that I know without a doubt. There is no one else but you for me. You help me to make my transfer from a harden criminal to a respectable member of society and for that I'm for ever grateful. You have never given up on me in times of uncertainty. For this reason, I shall forever cherish you. My love for you will last even after death, for all eternity.

To my childhood friends. Todd, Chris, Brian, Napolean, Joe, Larry, Mansfield, Miro and the rest of the 11th st posse, thanks for your support. And last but not least to David Moesley who has encouraged me to keep writing and to not give up. You have truly been a friend. I want you all to know that, I appreciate you. I appreciate all the get togethers, too!

burgundysoul@cox.net (comments)
David Leary (author) (602) 488-1929
Creator of Extreme Change, a new concept in dealing with the worst of the worse drug addicts.

A Letter to the Reader

Nothing that is false was added to this book in order to keep its legitimacy. However, the names were changed to protect the innocent. Anyone reading these stories will know for a fact that God is alive and prayers don't go unanswered. I pray that God forgives me. May he also, forgive me for the content of this book; however, I had to give it to you, the way it was given to me. In order to keep this book's legitimacy, I had to tell these stories exactly the way they were.

May the Lord bless the soul of Katherine Johnson, who died so unimaginably in the State of Arizona. This book is a special dedication to you.

This book was written with the hardest, of the hardest core drug dealers and drug abusers in mind. This book takes a true in-depth look at the real triggers of drug addiction. Perhaps for the first time ever, sexual addiction and drug dealing are thrown into the addiction equation. These are the things that were left out of the treatment phase, of drug addiction. So in a since, I was destined for failure. I did fail. This book was written by a former hardcore drug dealer and drug abuser.

The stories in this book are horrific and shocking, however, they must be told and heard to help in bringing about hope for the many more that chose to deal drugs, abuse drugs or just got caught up in the lure of drug addiction. This book is for the many that lost their souls and seek to have their souls restored. It is for the many that didn't have someone at home when growing up, to warn them that cocaine and meth kill. Anyone who brings pain to so many has to give something back, once their soul has been restored. If nothing else in life, I want to be forgiven for the pain that I have caused so many, and may God, also have mercy upon my soul. I want to be remembered not for what I was, but for who I am now. I know without a doubt that, my mother would be proud of me now, for what I'm trying to achieve. I'm finally the son she always wanted me to be. She just wouldn't get a chance to see it. It is the helping of a poor soul that may come from the power of this book that would make me proud. I could never seek glory for destroying lives. This is my contribution, to bringing about change.

When thoughts of doing drugs are in your dreams, there's almost nothing that can stop you from using, especially, if you loved the taste of these drugs like I did. Take it from someone who's been in the mud, who's been in the garbage. I was what you might call a human garbage can. I put meth, but mostly cocaine in my system daily and indefinitely with no restrictions. Before you can whip your opponent, you need to size him up. I recognize what it did to me before and ultimately, this destroys the urge, even at its strongest point. I want you to know that, when all hope is lost, it doesn't have to mean the end. If you ever contemplated suicide, there still is a cure.

No matter what, just don't do it." If I had followed the advice of the Beast while in a motel many years ago, this story would have never been told. I know what it's like to depend on my drug sales for my livelihood and to be locked in to this mindset with no way out. Selling drugs was all I did and this was all I wanted to do. I had no exit plans; I just kept selling dope, all the while knowing what it was doing to the people.

When God stepped in, he would demand my undivided attention and he would surely get it.

For me, going back to prison, was my destiny. When you get this far down in life, the only other place to go is about six more feet deep. After nearly destroying my life, I can honestly say that, any one can change. You must first have a sincere willingness to change and with the blessings of the Lord God Almighty, anyone can do it. If I can change, trust me, you can change too. In the process of writing this book, I came across all different kinds of characters in life: They were, just like me, the helpless, hopeless and mentally destroyed. If nothing else, it is my hope that, the message that's received from this book is heard. Hard drugs kill and destroy. If you are lucky to survive, it leaves painful memories which no doubt, last for a lifetime. This is my second attempt at writing this book and the first time publishing it. This book took a total of 15 years, to be brought into the light. For the ones who have been on the drugs for 20 years or more, don't give up. Don't let the Beast have the glory. Stay on your knees, my Lord God will comfort you. Your prayers will be answered. His word can't be void. These drugs destroy families and take lives daily. I know personally because, I saw it also destroy minds. Make no mistake about it, once you are addicted to the drugs, it's a fight for life, it doesn't make any difference whether it's cocaine, heroin, meth, or ecstasy and if you slip just once, death could be knocking at your door.

It's been sixteen years since my last use and I have to fight the drug cravings still from time to time. In those sixteen years, I have been clean from meth and cocaine's addiction, yet I still have the dreams, from time to time. The only difference between me and someone that uses is, I understand the battle that I am in. I know that I will continue to get the phone calls. I just don't have to answer and I don't. This is a fight that I must win; I will win, or die, not just my body but, also my soul. There's nothing in between. You have to make a choice. Make no mistake about it; I'm in a fight for the rest of my life.

This Is a True Story

This is the book that comes face to face
with the realities of the war on drugs.

Until the rules change, there can never be a winner.

CHAPTER 1

The Distinctive Difference

November 12, 1990, a date that is burned into my memory forever. Life as I knew it would never be the same again, ever. It was very hard to do, what I was about to do, but, when you are dealing with life, or death, the choice becomes simple. I was happy that I had awoken from the night that started with an ounce of cocaine and a fifth of Jack Daniels. Through the first quarter-ounce of the sack, my female companion left me. She was tired of my bullshit.

There I sat alone in the apartment. At this point in my life, I had lost all hope. It was at this point when I thought that the God that my mother reminded me about all of my life was not hearing my many prayers. Cocaine had a grip on my life for nearly ten years and there was nothing I could do at this point that could change things. There I sat, while reaching into my sack, pinching another rock of cocaine with a tight grasp of my fingertips while pushing powder up into my nose.

With each 15 minutes that went by, I continued the process of powdering my nose and then a stiff swallow of Jack Daniels. The police had been looking for me for over six months now. It was at this point, I had been up for four straight days. All my thoughts were irrational. All my logic was out the window. In my mind I wanted to die, I was tired of hurting and hurting all the people that came into my zone. There is a price to pay for what I had done, that would seem to be more then I could bear. As I sat there, all I could think of was death. My thoughts in my mind kept racing back and forth, *You are nothing but a fuck up, David. You are nothing but a fuck up, David.*

By this time in my life, I had sold dope for nearly 15 years, in which I had a network of somewhere around 200 clients. I lived by the name of Greedy D,

I lived by the theory of having the best dope. I sold dope 24/7 and I was willing to take it if need be and die for it if necessary. I was proud to be a dope dealer, this is all I wanted to do. The police had raided my houses at least twice and The Double Up Boys were in town, walking, selling dope on my turf. I needed to stop them, or so I thought at the time. In the end, I was my biggest client. I had started snorting cocaine and meth in 1982; it was just little lines at the time. Now I was snorting nearly an ounce of cocaine a day and I had overdosed at this point nearly ten times. Even worse, just one year prior, I was in the hotel with a gun pointed to my head, stressed out again to the max because, I had depended on the drugs for my total happiness and my total happiness is the one thing that would always be denied, while I was clinically addicted and insane.

My God was there with me once again, to see me through, I just didn't know it. Cocaine drove me, it pimped me, and most importantly, it nearly destroyed me. I had been in the clinics and drug treatment centers, and inpatient, and outpatient centers. I spent a year in the Arizona Family Drug Treatment Center. I remember these words as if they were part of the Bible: "Hi, my name is David, and I'm a dope fiend and I'm still showing dope fiend behaviors."

Another one was, "Hi, my name is David and I'm an alcoholic," "Hi, Dave." Also at this point, I had been sent to prison for 45 days to get my number, so that it would make processing easier, when I returned to the prison system. I would return indeed, for a six-year bid.

Prison for me, was my destiny. Even after all of this, nothing could help me, nothing would help me, or so I believed. From the governor of this great State of Arizona in the mid 80's to the wardens at each prison in Arizona, it was common knowledge among all that drugs were a major problem in the prison system and nothing has changed since and nothing has changed now. Some people actually check into prison and have no idea that this would be home forever.

When drugs hit my neighborhood in the early 80's, it destroyed family values and virtues and structures. The prison system would be no different. I would learn that the drugs would only come into the prison in two ways. They wore different color shirts, brown or blue, pick one. Back in those days, you would need a score card, to determine the players. All the clinics treated me for while I was on the streets was my addiction to drugs. However, there was no treatment for my sexual addiction and living the lifestyle of the big baller drug dealer. So, by the time I had gone to prison, I had gotten back into the drug business.

Back in those days, although it was called the Department of Corrections, it wasn't set up to correct you. This is why most people would come out, just as fucked up as when they entered. My sexual addiction was a behavior that interlocked with my drug addiction. This is a behavior that must be included in the recovery process. It can no longer be left out, or denied. I was so totally dependent upon cocaine for sex back in those days. I would place a mirror on some of the girls' backs, to snort lines while still in

*sexual rhythm. When I thought of cocaine, I thought
of sex. The more cocaine I would snort, the more
serious the cravings were for sex. I couldn't do one
without the other. I could not have sex without first
snorting some cocaine. This only enhanced the
thoughts of sexual arousal and emotions.*

*These parts were left out of the recovery
process. It's like putting out the fire; however, the
coal is still burning.*

I kept reaching into my sack and thinking, *How come
God, hasn't answered my many prayers? I'm going to die. You
are nothing but a fuck up, David.* Are the thoughts that kept
going over and over inside my mind. Yes, indeed, at this point
in my life I had become insane, as the message kept repeating itself inside my mind, *You are nothing but a fuck up,
David.* I couldn't stop putting the cocaine up my nose, even
as my heart beat violently. I had lost all touch with reality
once again. I started to hallucinate, and I was crying and hearing things. I was so high, I had been drinking all night and I
snorted so much while I was continuing to wonder, *Will this
be my last night on earth?*

With each pinch of the sack, my heart would beat violently, my body would sweat uncontrollably and I started to
smell. Yes, I had been there before, but then it was different
because I was alone. It was at this point, when I made an
agreement with God that, "If I could just wake up from this,
if I could just see another day again please dear Lord," was
my prayer. I began to pray to God again saying, "God help
me." "God help me." I knew death was near, while my heart
was racing, with each continued pinch of cocaine. Even
though I prayed, I continued to pack my nose with the
cocaine. I couldn't stop and I continued to drink. In my mind

the end was here. I was so close to death that I could feel it. The very next thing I could remember seeing as I woke up was the light glaring through the kitchen window and hearing the sound of people outside the door talking.

I looked down near my leg and there was the empty Jack Daniels bottle and the empty plastic bag. I had consumed the whole bottle and finished the whole ounce of cocaine. I knew, it was time to turn myself into the cops or I would surely kill myself, or even worse, someone else. I said to myself, "If God awakens me from what I went through last night, this will be my last and final night of using cocaine in meth."

How did I get to here? Most would find the answer to this question very, very, shocking and unimaginable and for sure, disturbing.

Nov 13, 1990: "David, stand against the wall, spread your legs and now stand over here so we can get your picture," the guard yelled. Once again, I was in the Horse Shoe at the Maricopa County Jail. The Horse Shoe is a motherfucker. Here you get a chance to look at society's rejects. It was there that I got a chance to look at people just like myself, who had lost all hope. Many, just like me, had burned all bridges. All had fallen from grace. I knew I was looking at a lot of time; after all, I was already on probation when I sold drugs to an undercover cop. I had gotten set up by someone who I thought was a friend. She lied to me and told me he was her cousin. Even though he looked to me like a cop, I sold the drugs to him anyway, trusting this friend. It was one of the things that we drug addicts do that comes back to haunt us. Unfortunately, mine came on my birthday. A year had passed by, however, somehow I knew this one would come back to bite me in the rear. This was the new charge. It came disguised in a certified letter called a secret indictment.

The old charges came from this guy that, I had gone to high school with, who brought the police to my house to witness the sale of cocaine. They never came into the house and they relied on this informant, Rolo, for all their information. Once the search warrant was signed, it was time for the police to invade my privacy; however, the police would run into one very, unexpected problem.

I had run out of dope right before the time they had gotten their search warrant signed. I was out of the drug, for a total of 10 days. The police would then give Rolo the informant, a half-pound of the drugs to give to me so that they could still raid my house, on a search warrant that was to have run out within seven days. Nearly six days had already expired. The police had to be the ones to give Rolo the drugs because they knew that I didn't have any and this is why they had not raided my house yet. They weren't aware that I had just scored a half-pound of the drug that morning about two hours before they raided, until Rolo left the house with the half-pound the police had given him. If I hadn't gotten the drug from my connection that morning, I would have taken the half-pound of cocaine from Rolo. Trust me no one can walk out of a house with a half-pound of pure cocaine while, a house is going to be raided in 10 to 15 minutes. This just doesn't happen because it's a crack house.

The police would apprehend anyone coming and going to this house especially if they were fixing to take this rock house down. No one could walk away from this house with that much dope, unless it was given to him, by the police themselves. I was going to get busted on this day, one way or another. The informant was with the police the morning they raided. There were just too many cops involved for them to come in and get nothing and to go back to the force empty handed. After all, it was somewhere around four different police agencies that would participate in this raid which would include the ATF, Glendale Police Dept Special Tactical Unit,

Phoenix Police Dept, Mary Vale Street Crimes Division. Like my mother always said, "What's in the dark will always come to the light?" They had to make sure I had the drugs because there were just too many police from different divisions involved in this raid. All this time, I kept wondering in my mind, how can they come in and get my drugs after 10 straight days of being out of the drug? They didn't have a wiretap. Had they had a wiretap, they would have gotten me over at Cowboy's house when I picked up the drugs, and they would have gotten him too.

They would also have known that Cowboy was a major player. They didn't know who Cowboy was and it was established in court that they didn't have a wiretap. Rolo was their eyes and ears. Cowboy didn't know when he would get more of the drugs so, it was also to his surprise that it would be on the same morning that the police were already going to raid me that he sold me drugs.

To make matters even worse, the search warrent was signed by a judge who would later get caught taking bribes in Arizona. This case was assigned to Honorable Judge Mar Fuci! Let me be the first to tell you that, there was nothing honorable about this judge! On the day of my sentencing for this crime, I will never forget his words: *"David Leary, don't you know that what you did was wrong?"* I then repeated, "Yes, sir, your honor," as his voice echoed through the court room. This judge would have no mercy. He then sentenced me! There was only one problem with this: the judge afterwards got caught coming in to an airport with some marijuana in his suit coat pocket. Like any common criminal, he had a good excuse saying, "Some Mexican had put it there," when questioned by authorities.

I have to give it to this judge, it made plenty of sense being that, he had just come from Mexico and he was a highly educated man. However, what would later happen would require prison time in which he would never serve! This very same Judge Mar Fuci would then get caught either attempting to mail a pound of weed through the U.S. mail or someone tried to mail the weed to the judge! Either way, this judge was no different than myself. This story was never ever mentioned again in the press to my knowledge. This judge would never do any prison time for this. When you are this far up in the power chain, secret deals are brokered. I know some guys, still doing prison time for using the U.S. mail to run drugs! I had to pay for the crimes, for what I did back then. It is now obvious to me that some of these law enforcement officials were above the law!

Although I was blinded to how it all went down back then, now I can see. I know now for sure, what had actually transpired back then. Now they can know that, I know exactly what they did; I know now that these cops violated the law in order to enforce the law. On this day, everyone included in the execution of this search warrant from the judge who signed it, to the cops who inforced it, to the judge who helped with the prosecution of it, had something to hide. I was Public Enemy Number 1. March 10 of 1987 will never be forgotten.

Think that this is impossible? This is only the beginning of a lot of the possibilities in this book, some of which would make the average reader say *no way, this cannot be possible*. But these things are real.

CHAPTER 2

A Step Backward

The Formation of Greedy D.

Paranormal: Meaning, impossible to explain scientifically.

I remember what my life was like at age five. Some people in their mid-40s would not remember their life back to this age. However, I do, for one reason and one reason only. I remember it so vividly because; I would get my first glimpse at paranormal activity. This day, like most any other day in Phoenix, Arizona, was extremely hot; however, this day would be different, much, much different, than all the days before this one.

I was outside playing in front of the house, with the red wagon that my mother had bought for me. My mom had the door cracked open so that she could keep an eye on me, while saying to me, "David, do not leave this front yard." While playing outside with the red wagon in front of the house, a man walked up from out of the blue. He startled me, I remember him so very clearly, because he just walked up and turned his head to the left in my direction and stared at me with those eyes that didn't look like they belong in anything human and his mouth opened wide, however nothing came out. He just stood there staring at me, with those eyes that looked like they weren't real and his mouth hanging open, when I jumped up and ran into the house to get Momma. He scared the living heck out of me. I began running toward the house yelling "Momma, Momma, Momma, there's this man outside Momma." I remember grabbing her hand, while leading her outside. When we get outside, this man would still be standing in front of the house, with that same look on his face, eyes bucked and still staring at me. I was pointing at this man, while saying, "See him Momma, see him Momma?"

Strangely, my mom would respond to me saying, "Boy, there isn't any man out here." I said, "Momma see, he's looking at me momma, he's standing right there looking." My mother would repeat herself again saying, "David, there isn't anyone out here, son. " I didn't know that at that very moment, I was seeing something that my mom could not see. Just as she repeated herself for the third time saying, "There is no one out here son." This man would then move out of the position that he seemed locked in, as he was staring at me. He would then turn his head to the right, and begin walking until he would disappear into thin air, just as quickly as he came. I would never see this man again, or know why he made his self known, only to me.

Most people wouldn't believe this and neither would I except, I saw him, looking at me, with those eyes that, didn't appear real. I will never forget him looking at me, with those eyes. I can tell you this one thing for sure, the things that happened in my life that, are hard to explain in life, would just keep happening. These things that would continue to happen to me would be hard for anyone to believe, who had no experience, in the supernatural.

Racism's Ugly Face

I remember at the tender age of eight, I didn't know that people hated me because of the color of my skin. Who could hate a little boy? I would soon learn that, it didn't matter if I was a little boy, or an adult.

I was Black and for that reason alone, I would be hated by many. I was one of five children and sometimes it would be hard for Mom to keep us all in her eyesight and that's

when, I would sometimes sneak off. Sometimes while walking up and down the street alone, older white men would pull up in their cars, while I was walking, trying to catch me. I was quick on my feet in those days and most of these men were fat and out of shape. I didn't know it at this time; however, they were also perverted. This would happen on at least three occasions that I could remember.

Each time, I would then run home and tell Momma about it. She would say, "That's why I tell you not to be walking up and down these streets alone, boy." She would then say that, "There are a lot of evil people in this world, son." I still didn't understand, what she meant by saying this. However, I was about to get my first lesson when in my classroom, here shown above at Monroe Grade School.

It would show that morning, once I had gotten to my classroom, just how much the color of my skin would make a difference. I remember talking in class, as the substitute teacher was talking. This would prove to have devastating consequences. He had warned me to be quiet. I should have heeded his first warning. As some kids do at this age, some don't listen, I was no different. It would have been very easy for him to just send me to the principal's office. The very next thing I knew was, the teacher was yelling at me and approaching me, while screaming at me. He was a white man, much bigger then I and intimidating. He just went off on me. Not even my behavior could justify what he did next to me.

The very next thing you know, my head was being rocked back and forth, from the barrage of punches, he was throwing. This teacher was hitting me in my face, like I was a man. He hurt me really badly. I started screaming, while running outside of the door of my classroom.

My nose was bleeding at the time and I was crying out loud, while sitting in the hallway. I was just outside the door and I had my head lowered and sobbing out loud when, I looked up and it was my sister, Cassandra. She said out loud, "What's wrong with you, boy?" I said to her, while weeping, "That teacher," while snot and a mixture of blood, was hanging out of my nose, "he was hitting me in my face." While still very teary eyed and trying to catch my breath. Her reaction was, "What?" "I'm calling Momma." When Momma came, she knew exactly what to do.

It didn't take my mother more then 10 to 15 minutes to get up to the school and we lived about 10 blocks away. Keep in mind we had no car. Momma would walk right past me, as I was crying in the hallway. She said nothing to me. I then followed her into the classroom; she was still in her housecoat, with her house shoes flapping in the air. Back then, Momma would stop whatever she was doing, if there was a problem with any one us. As the door was opened wider, she picked up speed, like a guided missile, being launched off the pad.

The very next thing you know, the teacher's eyes got extremely big as she approached him. As she unleashed her right hook, she said, "You don't be hitting on my son." For the moment, it made me feel better that someone would come along to avenge this senseless act. The other kids were amazed with what was taking place right before their eyes. In this classroom, everybody started yelling. At that very moment, she had made contact with the teacher's jaw, the teacher then took flight and slid across the floor and then got up and took off, running to the principal's office. I have to admit, Mom had a mean punch. Yet nothing would happen to this teacher for this and I do mean absolutely, nothing. I would see him at another school, three years later.

The Purpose

> *At this time in life, his mother was fighting this man for her son's dignity and respect. She didn't know if she could whip this man, she just knew one thing, nobody can treat her only son like this. Some 35 years later, unknowing to her son, it would be his turn to fight for his mother's dignity and respect. Like his mother, he wouldn't know if he could whip them, he just knew one thing for sure, nobody could treat his only mother like this.*

If this happened today, the bare minimum would be a firing and this teacher would never be able to teach at any school, ever again. More than likely, he would be arrested and taken to jail for child abuse. You don't do this to a kid. I was black and made to feel less than an inferior, from the

day I was delivered from the womb. Imagine being hated, and not even knowing why.

This picture above shows what it looked liked after the City of Phoenix was revitalized. It has received a face-lift, but back then, you only lived here if you were forced to live here. Hell lived here. We were a hated people, living near a hated environment of society called the East Side Projects.

I was raised up poor and I thought everyone was poor, well at least that's the way that it appeared to be in my neighborhood. Drugs and prostitution ran hand in hand and racism was evident.

This is the same house we lived in, but back then, it was a different scene. We stayed in many rundown houses, but this was the most memorable, because it was just so many rats, roaches and spiders. If you walked across the kitchen floors sometimes at nighttime, you would nearly step on a rat or hear the crackling of stepping on crunching roaches. When it rained, it rained inside as well. We stayed next door to the pickle factory, where the stench was ever so present. Every time we opened our front door, this would be the first thing you smelled. It would hit you in the nose, like the smell of walking up close to a skunk, in the middle of the woods. This was something that I just couldn't get used to. The pickle factory is no longer open; however, the memories will go on forever. The summers were so brutal, living in a house without an AC Unit, in Arizona. I remember many times sitting in my room during the summertime, with my shirt off, sweat pouring down my chest, as the swamp cooler blew only hot air because, its water pumps didn't work.

This Has Got to Be One of the Saddest Days of My Life

I was somewhere around the age of 9. I was so used to my mother being at home when I came home from school. So it was very unusual for my mother to not be home, on this day. As I approached the house from a long walk from school, I could see at a distance that, all my four sisters were standing or sitting on the front porch. As I had gotten closer to the house, I had noticed everyone with sad faces. As I walked up, I had already started crying, not even knowing what had happened. By the look on everyone's faces, I knew something bad had happened. I was then told by my sister Cassandra that, "Momma was at Kmart when she was arrested for shop lifting." Cassandra had then said, "Momma is in jail and she doesn't know when, she will be home." We all were in tears or somewhere near it because, we weren't used to our mother being gone from the house, much less being arrested. As the day started to become night, a sense of fear grew on everyone's face knowing that for the first time in our lives we were alone. Everyone was sobbing when all of a sudden a taxi pulled up in front of the house and it was Momma inside.

We all ran to the taxi, as Momma was getting out and yelled, "Momma, Momma!" Her first words were, "I'm okay." Once she had gotten into the house, I said to her with tears in my eyes, "Momma, what happened?" She then said this, "Son, I will never lie to you about anything because, I love you so much." She then said, "Son, I was so tired of not having enough money to buy you all new clothes. I'm so tired of only being able to afford to shop at thrift stores and I was so tired of you guys wearing hand-me-downs." She said, "Son, I just wanted you guys to have something new for school, that's all, son.

She then went on to say, "Son, when I told the security guard that I just was trying to get my kids something and that I was just so tired of being broke and not being able to afford you guys something new for school, he immediately let me go and didn't even call the police." She then went on to say "Son, I love you all so much that, I did something incredibly wrong. She said to me "Son, it's wrong to steal, and I won't do this again and don't you ever do it.

This woman lowered her morals and standards for her children. Back in these days, it was called survival and only the strong would survive and the weak would surely die. Nobody that lived here back then knew, or was prepared for what was headed our way. The Beast was coming and hell was coming with him.

I remember when I was around about 10 years old when, the government trucks came. The government would deliver food rationings to the poor. I ran down to the truck and asked them, could I get a job helping to unload the truck?" Once I had gotten done, the man stiffed me on my money. I didn't have a dad at home, so I had to go get the next best thing, Momma. My mom went up to the Truck with just her house coat on saying to me, "He's going to pay you." While pointing at me and then saying to the man, "He helped you didn't he? Then pay him." The Man then reached into his pocket and pulled out a dollar bill and gave it to me. My mother was willing to step up to the plate when need be, to play the role of my dad. Shortly after this incident, I remember the five of us walking with my mother. I remember some white guys yelling at us, while driving by, as my mother was walking with us. Sometimes, she would take the five of us and just go walking; this would also take our minds off how bad times really were.

It wouldn't take long sometimes for us to be reminded about how white people during those times truly felt about us. These white guys would pull up, in what looked to be a fast car. While throwing bananas at us, while saying, "Eat the bananas, you fucking monkeys." I remember my mother saying, "You all better go on and leave us alone," and then looking back at us and assuring us while saying, "We are going to be okay." As a kid, I didn't understand why these people hated us. I would later learn, this was a common thing. Directly across the streets from us, were the Projects.

Van Buren Street

This is the street that the hoes and the pimps controlled. This was the street that was heard of in just about every state. If a pimp was working Arizona with his hoes, he would be working Van Buren. At any given time you would see at least a hundred hoes working these streets. At nighttime that number could double. Or even triple.

I would commonly see used condoms, stretched out nearly everywhere I walked. Pimps circled the blocks making sure their hoes were taking care of business. The pimps would come from just about every state, to work the streets of Van Buren. This was the strip. Nothing like Las Vegas, a lot like the ghetto. There was one pimp, out of the many that came to Arizona that I will never forget, for a couple of reasons. One was that, once he came down here and played with the big boys, he was then forced to leave, not by his own will, but in a casket. They called him Moose.

Moose came down to Arizona from Texas and made these Arizona pimps go back to the drawing boards. A few Arizona pimps were still walking and trying to be a pimp. Imagine this one. Most had old Cadillacs, or old Lincolns. Some of the Arizona Pimps hadn't seen anything like this brother. He had a Cadillac that was out of this world, for back in the days. He wore a big gold plate on his chest, the first that I had ever seen that was in big solid gold letters that said, MOOSE.

This was big pimping. This brother was representing the State of Texas to the utmost. This brother had diamonds or gold on every finger. This pimp had real hoes from different races. This brother was doing the most business in my opinion.

Arizona pimps hadn't seen anything like this before so naturally, it would be resented. I met him one day while, washing his big pretty Cadillac. My car club was out trying to raise some money that day when he came to support us. Every time you saw this brother, he was flashing hundred dollar bills. This wasn't common then. His was the first Caddy that I saw with some curtains in it.

I was just a teenager back then and looking at this guy, he looked like he was living the life and I wanted to be just like him.

Moose wasn't ready for Arizona and Arizona wasn't ready for the Moose. Somewhere around eight months later, Moose would get his ass shot up and then he got robbed, for all his gold and diamonds. They say, when he was shipped home, he had nothing on him. If he had known that Arizona would literally suck all the life out of him, he would have stayed away from this state. *Sometimes it can appear that you are winning, but you could actually be losing.*

This is where the people's sufferings were also evident. Directly behind us was another rundown apartment and an alleyway where, tricks would bring their Johns, for fifteen minutes of pleasure. You could catch more than sex being

displayed here then. This is also where the pimps would beat down the whores who were short on their pay.

Although things have changed here now, the memories remain the same. There where fights nearly every other day in the projects, most times between kids and sometimes between parents.

I remember just getting out of juvenile and my mom bringing me to this house and I was crying to her saying, "Mom, I don't want to live here," and her responding, "Son, I can't do any better, so this is where we have to stay." It was hard for her, it was even harder for me, when other kids would make fun of her because, she wore rags and clothes that she had handmade, she would just say, "You all better go on, I'm going to tell your parents." My mother didn't have much and she gave us all she had. I hated these kids for this.

You could mess with me, but not my mom. I was powerless to do anything often; there were more of them than me.

"This was a living hell no doubt about it. My mother wore rags, in order for us to have, and what we had was all she could give. We were happy because we knew, she was doing her best. She used to say to me, 'Son, I can write a story of my life.'"

She would never get a chance to write it. She could not have known at this time that, the story would still be written, but not by her and more than some 35 years later.

We were living right in the middle of a living hell and the odds of us making something positive of our lives, were slim to none. They had taken me to Juvenile because, I had snatched a white woman's purse and not long before, I had jumped on a white kid, after watching *Roots* on television the night before. I broke his nose with one punch; he was a big kid, even bigger than me. I thought he would fight back, but he didn't. Later, three white cops had paraded me across Phoenix Union High School Campus, in handcuffs once they had caught up with me, while all my classmates watched in disbelief. They then took me downtown, to the Police Department and then into a room where, no one else could see. One of the three cops kept edging on the others, to join in on the ass whipping he wanted to give me. He kept saying, "Yeah, he hit a white kid." I thought for sure they would beat me down. They didn't however, they contemplated it and that was enough to scare the living hell out of me.

This was only what happened at the end of the day. There was a gang of about 5 of us who just went around hitting as many people as we could—enraged by this TV show the night before. This is how the morning really started out.

Everyone was upset after watching the treatment of black people, just because of the color of their skin. After being called nigger almost daily by cops and members of my society and made to feel less than and unequal, one could somehow become bitter as a kid. In my mind as a teen, the police were the enemy. Back then, they were part of the problem and not the solution, no doubt about it.

My mom tried to do her best with the five us and then the sixth child would come. He was my nephew. My nephew was dropped off recently, in my mother's arms and my mother loved him like I, her only son. She would say he is your nephew, David, but he is also your brother. My mother only received $140 a month from the government and at one time we ate state-issued cheese and spam, powdered eggs and powdered milk. "Government raised, no doubt."

Momma could handle people being mean to her, but she wasn't going to let any one hurt us, especially me, because I was her only son. No matter the direction my mother guided us in, the future never looked promising to us, from my very own viewpoint, it didn't look promising at all. She taught us not to hate, even though we were hated for the color of our skin, and I just couldn't understand this, especially as a kid. I was right out of juvenile, finally at home; however, the stress of just living over here was taking its toll.

I often would wonder, "Why did we have to live like this, and who is this God that, my mother prayed to so often?" My mother was a God-fearing woman, who sent us to church when she couldn't attend. On Sundays, you better not touch the radio, when Sunday Services were on. If you did, in the blink of an eye, her house shoe would already be in flight. We walked everywhere, and she never owned a car.

To make things better, from time to time I would stick my speakers out the door and play music and believe it or not, this actually brought peace to so many who, were in a living hell. They say music soothes the savage beast. We weren't beasts; however, after doing these hard drugs, some of us acted like it. People would be driving by, or walking by and they would start either dancing, or popping, or snapping their fingers to the beat, with a smile on their face.

At one point this would be requested by the neighborhood kids, who had became accustomed to hearing the music from the 70s, and then the kids would roller skate in bunches, up and down the sidewalk in the Projects. Those were the happier times. Along with the drugs, you would see pimps riding by in their tight ass cars, looking for their hoes.

These were really just some of the times that, our minds were taken off of the daily struggles we faced, yet struggling would be only part of the equation. My mom started me out as a good kid; I took up the martial arts, karate and judo. I went to the Boy's Club, and I even took up weightlifting. This is a picture of me competing, with some of the other Sweat Hogs.

I used to be a member of the Butler's Boy's Club Sweat Hogs. We competed with other Boy's Clubs, all over the valley in weightlifting championships. I'm the one sitting at the right end, near my coach and his wife. I respected this man because, he didn't play the race game. Sometimes he would actually come to my house, to get me for the events. He was also the one who let me know that all cops weren't bad because, he was also a cop. I will never forget this man. He taught me that all white people are not bad either.

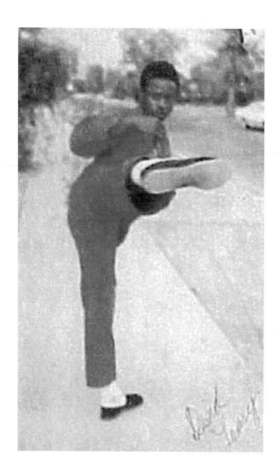

My mom did the best she really could, in times that were unfavorable for her and us. She just didn't know, or wasn't aware that, there was nothing that she could do for me. She made me go to church on Sundays. I was strong back then as a kid, but not strong enough to fight off the power of evil, wickedness, hatred, and bigotry.

I would later get stabbed while at the Boy's Club. I remember the director of the Club, telling me while at the

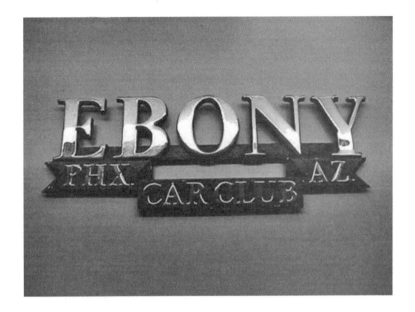

hospital to get stitches, "Don't tell anyone who stabbed you at the club." But he wasn't the one who was bleeding.

I started the second black low-rider car club in Phoenix, Arizona called the "Ebony Car Club." This is a picture of one of the plaques that we flew near our back windows in our cars. I really tried my best to get my life back on track; however, it would seem that my destiny had already been decided for me. My mother actually guided me in the right direction, but her best would not be good enough. Nothing would prepare me for what I was about to face in life. As a kid, going without meals sometimes and growing up in a drug-infested neighborhood. This could somehow take a mental toll on anyone. The seen was, pimps chasing down whores in their brand new Cadillacs. How much worse could it get? It gets much worse.

My mother never lost her faith in her God and taught us all to pray when times got rough. Needless to say, my mom prayed nearly every day because, times were rough. In the end, I found this to be a very useful tool. I stole food from this store below, to help my mother feed us, I would later get caught doing so. I had to reach in my pants and I had to give back the package of ham, before I could make it out the door. I was then warned by the Chinese man who said, "Don't come back in this store." This man would have no understanding— I was just hungry. It was at this point, I would need a father figure at home.

My dad would come in get me and take me from time to time to work with him. I had also got a job with him in the summer, doing construction work. My dad was a good man. He too would have to battle many injustices in life himself. He worked hard in the heat doing construction work, mostly digging holes with a hand shovel. He worked five to six days a week. He never owned more than his car.

He didn't live with my mom so during this time, I would probably see him once every two weeks or more. I really needed this father figure at home; maybe I would have turned out differently, maybe I could have had at least a 50% chance of making it? Maybe, I would have had a better chance to succeed in the path of something wicked, this way comes. Everything in its path would be mentally damaged or destroyed.

At the present, the neighborhood was deteriorating fast; hard drugs had entered our domain. These drugs would prove to take the people's suffering to a new height. People would dip cigarettes in sherm, which has embalming fluid in it, and then sale them for $10 to $20. I used to see people smoke this stuff and lose their fucking minds. Some would strip down to bare naked and run around acting a fucking fool. Others would go into a zombielike state and sometimes wouldn't return. This was some bad stuff, keeping it real.

This was only the beginning, for the worst was still to come

When the worst came, it came with total devastation and mental anguish that would destroy lives, for many years to come.

It was hard to see as a kid some of my friends' moms hooked on this and then walking around looking mummified.

Most kids were like me and didn't have a father figure around. I used to watch some go into a yelling like frenzy and just start crying without stopping. You think you got it rough? It gets tougher. I used to watch some who would break nearly every window out in their apartment and then run out of the rental unit screaming, while taking off all their clothes and then continue yelling and screaming. Picture this being your momma, your sister, or your friend? You would think that being extremely poor and hated by whites was enough back then. But being poor and hated was only the beginning.

By the 80s, Sales of Cocaine Became a Billion-Dollar Enterprise

Cocaine was coming to our neighborhood. Sherm, would have to take a backseat. The destroyer was in our neighborhood. Total devastation, destruction and death came with it. One family at a time and sometimes many families would fall to the lure of this drug sometimes overnight. I would be no different. Many would start off by selling it and once ingested, would be pimped by it. Sometimes you would see a pimp, whipping on a hoe right in public. When cocaine came to our neighborhood, it took over the pimping game as well. It was hard for a pimp to get paid because, most pimps that I knew at this time, had gotten smoked out as well. Now the pimp was getting pimped.

I used to hear on the TV set, of someone committing suicide from drugs and at this point I couldn't understand why. I remember asking my mother, "Why would people commit suicide?"and she didn't really have an answer. I would later find out firsthand because, trouble was headed my way, full throttle.

In 1981, I met Cowboy. He moved directly across from me and he just had been released from prison. Cowboy had long hair and tattoos every where. Cowboy immediately was into the chips; in other words, he was making a lot of money. I would see him coming and going. He started buying different cars and it didn't look like he worked anywhere. He didn't associate with many people; however, he would nod his head to me from time to time, as he would go by.

I also met my second girlfriend—Clarisse. She would later change my thoughts about the typical girlfriend. Clarisse played me like a piano and used and abused my feelings. She was some kind of freak. I was naive about how some women could be. In other words, I was vulnerable when I met her back in the days. My mother was also a girl and I had four sisters. She taught me to respect all women. I thought all girls were nice and the same, I would never be so wrong. Clarisse took advantage of all my weaknesses and she was a nympho-maniac. I didn't know what that term meant—at that time and she taught me real fast. Clarisse was the type of girl that one man could never satisfy sexually. No matter how much I would try, I just couldn't do it. To make a long story short about Clarisse, I was in love with her, or so I thought. She was basically sexing her ex and his cousin and me at the same time, and sometimes in the same room.

Clarisse was a beautiful, chocolate-dark girl, who had a body that would make an old man want to pay for it and trust me plenty did. Just that walk she had, in the short white pants and white halter top, she could stop a car in the middle of traffic and she was some kind of freak. The only problem with this at the time was, I didn't know about it.

Her hips swung side to side, as she walked by. She would make it a point to do daily walks and guys would just look at her with hopes of some type of relationship. Yes indeed, this girl had a serious body. She hurt my feelings and made an ass out of me in front of my Car Club Members on the same day. One night, while getting home from work late, around 12 pm, I was in front of Clarisse's house looking for her. The fellows and I were standing around her front door. Some of them had smiles on their faces, as if they knew something that I didn't. Clarisse's ex-boyfriend just stayed above her.

Some of the guys were trying to warn me saying before this, "Clarisse is a nasty bitch," however; I couldn't see this. What's the term? I wasn't at the time, quick on my feet. The song "Freaks come out at night." would become true. Clarisse came out of his apartment, hair all nappy and just walked right by me and the fellows and went into her house. This just blew me away. I couldn't sleep that night, all I could picture in my mind was, seeing her come out of his door. This scene would be repeated in my mind, every single time I saw her, after this day for years to come. The very next day, this same girl came over and wanted to apologize for what she thought was just a misdemeanor, she wasn't serious at all. She just didn't know that, I viewed this act as a class one felony. She made an ass out of me. The next day, I still thought everyone was laughing at me. That day, I had her giving me oral sex and she had never done it before, well at least not to me. This was only the beginning. I made her walk the corner; I needed her to prove her love for me. I had become a pimp that next day and it would end that same day.

I remember her crying while standing on the corner saying, "Why are you doing this to me?" I hit her in the face at least a couple of times, yelling at her while saying, "Bitch, don't be crying on this corner hoe," I then said to her, "I was taking you out to eat and to the movies, I brought you new clothes, trying to show you how much I respected you, I treated you like a woman, when this nigga cares less." I then said, "This nigga don't spend a dime on you, and you're fucking him and his cousin." Again I would say "Don't be crying on this corner hoe." I then said to her "Bitch, I'm going to show you how to fuck." I would not let her down, on this promise. I had remembered seeing this one pimp go upside his hoe's head one day, in the back alleyway while taking out the trash one early morning, so I thought, this would be the correct instrument to use at this time. Not only this, but growing up as a kid, I watched my dad sometimes hit on my mother when he was drunk. I was wrong.

Shortly afterwards, a big cop would pull up. He never said anything to Clarisse, and he had only a few words to say to me. He said to me, "Look here man, I'm going to make this block and you better be gone." I started up the car and left immediately. Clarisse started walking up the street; I wouldn't see Clarisse again until the next day. But that day, my mother went off on me. I remember those words today. "David, what the hell's wrong with you?" She then said, "Are you losing your damned mind boy?" She then went on to say, "Leave that girl alone boy and I mean that." One thing about Momma, when she said she meant it, that's exactly what she meant. Remember, Momma had a serious right hook too. I would see Clarisse the next day and I was saddened after seeing her face. One side was extremely large. I then said to her, "I was very sorry for what I did, but you must understand that you hurt me. I was in love with you." The next thing I did was, I shared her with at least three of my Car Club buddies over time and then one of my friends at work and then one guy from the Arizona Family Drug Treatment Center. This would go on for years to come.

To make me feel better for the next eight years, I shared her with my buddies and people I just had met; we would both have sex with her. Sometimes when I would share her with a friend, she would say "I love you, David, and I'm trying to show you." But there was nothing she could do to make me stop hurting. This type of three way sex with her, actually made me feel better, when I thought about what had transpired back in the day. I felt when a person screwed me over I had to do them ten times worse. It was this incident that would change my thoughts about some women for years to come.

Cowboy would later turn out to be one of the top drug dealers and I would become his instrument, delivering drugs to the black and white and brown community. One day, I bought three stolen shotguns for $175 dollars. I was looking for a buyer when, Cowboy drove up. I said to Cowboy, "Hey man, how are you doing?" He said, "Cool, what's up?" I then said, "Hey man, you got any need for any guns?" I then saw his face light up, like a slot machine, when he said, "Sure, what kind do you have?" I then showed him and he replied, "Would you trade for marijuana?" I said, "Cool."

Little did I know it, it was at this very moment, we were forming a relationship that would last somewhere around 11 years and millions of dollars would pass through our hands. However, along with the excitement and the euphoria, came unbearable pain and agony and anguish which would nearly destroy my life and many more lives in its path. After trading Cowboy the guns for the weed, I then quickly sold the quarter-pound of weed.

I realize at that point, there were a lot of people who liked it. The next thing you know, I was selling pounds and I started to build my network. People began to depend on me for it. Nobody knew that I got all my weed from Cowboy. He and I kept quiet about it and we became tight. Cowboy always showed some interest in Clarisse; whenever he would come over during this time. He would be talking to me but looking at Clarisse. One day I would use this as leverage.

Now, The Destroyer Would Be Introduced

Cowboy yells at me one day while standing on his porch, "Hey Cowboy." which was the term we called each other. He then said, "Man, come on over here right now." Once I had gotten to his door I said, "What's up?" He said, "Hey man, you ever do Coke before?" I said "No man, but I've heard about it." He said, "Try a line, this is some real good shit."

I used a straw that was already on the mirror, which he just had used in front of me, to let me know that, it was okay. I did two lines, "Man that's strong Cowboy," I replied. Cowboy repeated his self when he said, "This is some really good shit." It made me feel real good, also bolder. *Later it would become a necessity before, during and after sex.*

Cowboy had called me over to his apartment, at least on three more occasions to offer me cocaine, for free. At this time I thought that, he was the greatest thing to happen to me. I could have never been so wrong. He knew what he was doing to me at the time; the only thing I knew was that it was real good and all I wanted was more. I remember seeing Cowboy outside at his apartment, and I yelled to him "Hey cowboy, you got any more of that shit?" he said "Yeah, but now, you need to start paying for it." I cashed him out and then beamed up to see Scottie, a term meaning, I was higher then a mother fucker.

The very next thing you know, I was buying it from Cowboy on a daily basis. The more I did of these drugs, the more unstable I became and the bolder I became.

This guy whom I idealized, he was an ex-con and he seemed to me to be the coolest. Actually he was a monster, who stole my innocence; he robbed me of my values and beliefs, he basically pimped me. It was during this time, I truly needed a father figure around and Cowboy took advantage of the situation. He was what every parent should fear. He knew what he was doing by introducing me to cocaine. He knew he would be able to control me and most importantly, he knew that he could make money from this type of control and making money is exactly what we did.

To make things even worse, the movie Scarface
*had been released and in our neighborhood, all
hell had been unleashed with it.*

Somewhere Around June 1985

Cowboy and I both moved out of the Projects. We had begun to make a lot of money in the drug trade. I also worked at the time for Motorola, on 52nd and McDowel. Most every one I knew smoked weed at Motorola, during this time. I would say 80% of the employees got high. I sold just as much weed at Motorola, as I did in the Projects.

I remember one day doing a big weed deal in the bathroom at Motorola when my boss walked in at the end of the deal. I was still counting money that was being picked up off the sink. He had also seen the bag in which the marijuana was in, or so I thought? He came in and looked at me very strangely. He would look at me with his eyebrows arched, which immediately let me know he wasn't happy at all. It was during this time, I would come into work sniffling every day, from my constant powdering of my nose with cocaine. Employees would ask from time to time, "It seems like your colds never seem to go away?" Sometimes while in conversations with people at my Job, my nose would bleed without warning. Just like that, blood would start pouring out of my nose. This same boss would later demote me and question me asking, "Are you dependent on drugs?" At the end of my stay at Motorola, I was making a lot of money. I had a guy who worked in the Gold Department, who was stealing Motorola's gold and then trading it to me for weed.

The first time he gave me the gold, it was in chips; it had been carved out of one of the gold layer spraying machines. This guy gave me my first bag and told me it was gold. I didn't believe him, but later after taking this sack to the gold buyers and being paid $500 for it, it was clear to me what it was. Even Dawanna laughed, when I showed it to her saying, "That isn't gold." But after being paid the money, she was wondering when I would get more.

She knew I had only given him an ounce of weed which was valued at the time at 40 bucks and I just made $500; there would be laughing no more. Eventually I would be fired for violation of the attendance policy, but not before cashing in a lot of gold and selling a lot of weed to employees.

It was hard going to work after a night of being up all night, from the sex and the drugs. The meth kept me up and on point for days. Five years at Motorola came to an end. A good share of my profits had come to an end as well. Cowboy and I moved our operation to North Phoenix while keeping soldiers in position in the Projects, to continue making profits. Then the unexpected happened.

The Double Up Boys were in Arizona

The Double Up Boys were in Arizona and they didn't come this far to fill out an application for a job.

The Double Up Boys from California came to Town; it was somewhere around 100 of them at first, then that number grew. They were going from South, East, to West, taking over our drug turfs. They were beating down people I knew and in some cases shooting them. I couldn't believe what was happening. In all my life of criminal activity, or just plain old being alive, I had never seen anything like this before. These guys from California were just going to come to Arizona and "De Bo," or take over, our turf. I was saying to myself at that time that, they don't come here with that cowboy shit and take my money." I started stacking up on my weapons, my favorite the AK-47, "Yes," this would be the tool. They were well organized and their product was twice as big as mine and cheaper and better—at least, this is what the smokers thought.

This is why they were called the Double Up Boys because, you could get double. "Bob," my soldier in the hood called me one day and said, "Hey Greedy D, you got to come see this mother fucking shit." A lot of people give themselves nicknames, but a true nickname came from other people. They had started originally calling me Greedy D because, I had a

huge desire to bed as many women as I could find. I was doing so much cocaine at this time that, I had become sexually addicted to cocaine. Meaning I couldn't perform sex without doing cocaine.

I craved the sex and the drug at the same time. It was also at this time that, I would have sex in eight-hour sessions. While on meth I could perform for days. The most ever was five days and when I was done, I had to go check in to the hospital for a drug overdose. This is why I had the need to sex as many women as I could, because, I would ware one out sometimes as many as three, and then be somewhere on the prowl for the next.

The term Greedy D, would change when, I started putting a heavy hand down for the dope sack. I was one of the few drug dealers from whom you could purchase a $10 rock and also a $45,000 kilo. Most drug dealers sold just twenties and up to a ½ ounce at a time, back in these days, that I knew. But not Greedy D, I would be getting the dimes as well. I wouldn't let much get by.

Bob called and told me, "There's got to be somewhere around one hundred of them, meaning the Double Up Boys, with drug shops all over our neighborhood and they are just selling it right on our corner, out in the open." Bob went on to say that, "They got the drive-through going on and they got guns." He said, "They just took over."

"Drive on over here right now and see this shit man, right now Greedy, man." he would say. This picture above shows the exact corner that the Double Up Boys had the drive-through up and operational. They weren't trying to hide anything, they were trying to make a statement. It would appear the way that the Double Up Boys were making their money on this corner, that the Police were afraid of the Double Up Boys. Nonetheless, when the California Boys came here and put a heavy hand down, they were making ends meet like a mother fucker.

I picked up Bob and I drove through the neighborhood, in disguise because, at this point I had gained a little status as a drug dealer. I was real proud of myself at this time. Once we had gotten there, it was just how Bob described it to be. People were in a zombie like state saying, "I'm going to see the Double Up Boys, they got double."

Whatever the mixture that was in their dope, it had one ingredient in it that was making people lose their fucking mind. Sometimes they were in groups of two or more, walking by you saying, "I'm going to see the Double Up Boys, they got double." The scene was almost out of a comic book.

I just had not witnessed anything like this before. Mothers were renting out their apartments to the Double Up

Boys for crack and giving up their cars. Bob even bought some, so I could see the size and what the hype was all about. Bob then took a hit. The next thing you know, his eyes were all big and shit. The brother was looking all around and shit. I'm looking at him at this time saying, "Hey man, you all right nigga." He then repeated these words, "Yeah man," eyes all bucked and shit, he was talking to me however, he wasn't looking at me.

The next thing you know, my drug sales started to bottom out, every one was buying from them, even my customers were buying from them saying, "I'm going to see the Double Up Boys, they got Double."

Things started to really get bad for my business. The thing that every big baller hates. I had been knocked down in status a peg or two. I had to go back to the front lines. I had to go back to where I had made some of my money which was on the street corners. I was out of work and in out of my mind. I had to get the money the best way I could, or so I thought. One thing was for sure, Greedy D knew how to get that money.

I had to go back to the basics because at one point no one was calling my pager. Bob, Perry, and I started tapping into new territory. We moved our dope business to the south side. "Good, the Double Up Boys just left," I had said to Bob. We were on 25, on Broadway Street, with our guns for the Double Up Boys, if they got out of hand while drinking, laughing and selling dope.

Bob started yelling out loud, as the customers would come by. "Get your Boo yaw, Boo yaw, get it while it's hot, we got that killa right here man, Boo yaw, Boo yaw, right here baby." This went on all night. Bob had me laughing all night, with that shit. Bob was a character and one of the funniest back in the days, no doubt about it. Bob also had Greedy D attributes and he was willing to stay on that corner all night with me, to get that money man.

He was also someone that I depended on, if shit got out of hand. Perry, what I liked about this guy is, he had heart. Like me, he wasn't afraid to kill someone. He also didn't mind packing a pistol and using it like me and 1 felt at that time, he would be a good asset to have around. I felt my boys had to be just as tough as I was, or tougher. Needless to say these guys fit my profile. It started to get hard to sell anything in my own neighborhood, damn. They had the dope game locked down; the Double Up Boys were doing a full court press. For the moment, they were getting mostly all of the money. Even worse, I was starting to like my own dope a little more. I was not following one of the three rules as said in the movie *Scarface,* when Tony Montana had said, "Don't get high on your own supply." I idolized this character. I found myself becoming more addicted to cocaine and sex. I couldn't do one, without the other. Richard Pryor described how good cocaine really was, while having sex better than anyone I know. He said, "I'm going to run around the house three times and on the third time, I want you to jump off on my face."

The nosebleeds continued to get worse, especially if I did crystal meth. This shit kept me up for days, I had done just a small amount at first. Unlike cocaine, it would take a lot less to get the same results. Bob and I, or I and Perry would lure women in, with the promise of the drug and the promise they could get high all night, if we could get ours and then we would have what we would call tag team sex. While one guy was having sex with the girl, the other would be waiting one foot away and naked and on point, to be tagged in. This drug was unlike nothing we had ever experienced. Once you had gotten a girl hooked on it, she would then basically be your sex slave. This is what I did to Clarisse, I would at first have to force it down her nose and later on there would be no force required, this is how I got Clarisse hooked on it in the beginning.

The morals for women who used this stuff were out the window, so to speak. I knew plenty of girls who were raised up in loving environments, but when they had got all strung out on this drug, they would give you oral sex for a $10 rock. You didn't even have to know them. Just pull up, and take it out. Imagine this being your momma and she's fucked up on this shit. This stuff is really fucked up. Think this isn't still happening? Think again.

I was experiencing more with meth, since it is the only drug that would keep you up for days with just a little bit, $25 worth to be exact. When I couldn't find cocaine, meth had to do. The sex was even more unreal with meth. While using it, I would be like a Trojan horse for days. This was definitely more powerful than cocaine. If used together, the possibility of dying became an immediate reality.

The very next thing you know, I wasn't paying my dope bill in a timely manner with Cowboy, I had been getting a lot of dope from Cowboy and not paying the bill at the end. I started talking Cowboy out of more and more dope, without paying my bill in its total, I would always owe him hundreds at the end of a deal, with the promise to make it up on the next deal, that would never happen. Cowboy was now looking for me.

I remember coming home that day, asking my then girlfriend, Dawanna, "Has Cowboy been here?" and then she said, "He just left, not only that, but he keeps calling. What's up?" I told her, "I owe him and I don't have the money to pay him and he's not happy." I was ducking and dodging Cowboy, trying to buy time, to pay him his money. I was stressed out at this point and nearly broke and doing as much of the drug as I could. Just one month prior I had 40 pounds of weed and about a kilo of cocaine. Now I was broke and all the bills were due.

This is when I would soon experience my very first drug overdose. This is when I had the 40 pounds and the kilo. Little did I know that this would be the very first of a series of drug overdoses to come. I will never forget it because, after being up all night doing cocaine, my heart started beating irregularly (I was scared because it was hard to breathe). I was scared shitless when the ambulance showed up at the front door with a City of Phoenix Police Officer.

I wasn't expecting them to come to my house, with the cops. That made my heart beat even more rapidly because, he was asking me questions about how much dope I did. I still had a lot of weed and cocaine in the house. He was looking all around, and thank God, he didn't go into my closet because that's where all the drugs were.

Cowboy probably came around three or four more times and called. After not being able to reach me successfully, he stopped coming by and calling. Cowboy didn't pursue the matter anymore, he just cut me off, no more communication. We had a mutual amount of respect for each other that went beyond the drug business at this time. The next thing you know, I was broke and had no way of getting more drugs from Cowboy, nor did I have any way of paying my bills.

I then tried to get my girlfriend, Dawanna, to get a job and help pay some of the bills with no luck; I couldn't get her to keep a job more than a couple of weeks. She was just living with me with no intentions of getting a job, or keeping one. What could I expect, after all; when I met her, she didn't have a job. I never heeded my mother's first warning, "She wouldn't be the right girlfriend to have, son." Needless to say she was sucking me dry. She was high maintenance.

CHAPTER 3

Action Jackson's

Jacking, starting out on a small scale. However, I would eventually take it full scale, full throttle. This is how Bob described it, "Jacking started with the smokers, who would drive up in their cars and ask to see the dope. The drug dealer would then stick his hand in the car and the smokers would then hit the bottom of his hand, the rocks would then fly up into the car and the smoker would then hit the gas and take off, with all the drug dealer's dope." They would come two weeks later and repeat the same process. This is how jacking came to be. Bob described actually seeing this happen, on more than one occasion, while we were powdering our nose on a street corner, selling dope. I remember Bob saying, "It was time for Action Jackson."

Bob said, "It's time for Greedy D to start putting his pistol in people's faces, man, it's time to start getting paid man." He then said, "Greedy they will give up the money, with the Clint Eastwood sticking in their fucking face." Bob said these "California boys, are making all the money and now it's time for Action Jackson, our motherfucking selves, baby." Bob started describing how he had already done this at least once. He said, "It paid pretty well."

While Bob was speaking, I was thinking to myself, *Yeah, but not at gas stations and stores where your chance of getting caught is somewhere around 80%.* I was thinking of jacking other drug dealers, who don't call the cops in 99% of the cases. In my mind, these would be easy victims for the jack moves. I could have never been so very wrong.

Bob kept encouraging me to start jacking. He said, "This is the way to get Cowboy to start helping you because you would be able to pay off the bill with him and be put back on the map all at the same time."

I didn't know it but when Action Jackson's was put in motion, this would change the dope game forever. When the jack move had gotten popular, a good number of people in the dope game were doing it.

It was nothing like having a free kilo of dope and in the end, I had plenty of them. It was also nothing like some very upset motherfuckers looking for you when finding out for sure that you jacked them. This could have undesirable consequences. At this point, I could only see the good side of it. However in the beginning, I had to start somewhere. I ended up jacking my first victim, a guy who worked at Motorola with me.

I felt bad about it; however, I was broke and at that time, I wasn't to be denied. First I went over to buy the dope. I had bought from him several times before, twenty here, twenty there. Then I ended up figuring where he was keeping his stash, so later that evening, I gathered up a couple of my soldiers and we went and handled business. I thank God that I have never killed anyone. However, I had to show these people that I meant business. So usually, I came with an overwhelming display of force. I would later learn how to outsmart you to receive the same results, but for now, I was new to the business. Usually I would display my 45 Smith & Wesson, but in this case, we just went to where he last put it in the backyard and it was there. The three of us jacked, for almost an ounce of cocaine, which was all he had, so we ended up splitting it up three ways. The guys that helped me with this started smoking theirs with the bitches and then they would be broke again, but not Greedy D.

Being that I was already down and out, I had to sell mine to come back up. At this point in my life, I had moved in with one of my sisters. She lived in Maryvale which was far west from where we had grown up. She would always say to me, "Bro, if you need a place to stay, you could come out here." It was cool because, she let me take over the house. She was kind of helpless in the matter because she was barely making ends meet and she needed some help. She really didn't know what she was doing by offering me a place to stay, at this point in my life. She let me open up shop.

To be honest she really didn't have a choice. She needed my help and I had grown in size and just the mere sight of me was intimidating and my behavior wasn't by any means normal. Little did I know Maryvale would in a sense, become all of mine. Maryvale at the time was untapped territory, for major players like me.

I would soon take over all of Maryvale in my mind, with the drug trade and set up a new customer base, which would be stronger and larger than the previous. The first order of business was to get rid of this girl, Dawanna.

Dawanna also had a boyfriend in prison, to whom she would sometimes send some of the bill money. Money and drugs would come up missing. This girl was sucking me dry. She started to become real heavy. Most guys would be weak, for a shot of ass and a pretty face; most would have kept her around. I felt that as long as I kept narcotics around, a pretty girl would be a dime a dozen. I just wish, I would have thought of this in the beginning. Sometimes, it would seem that Dawanna liked pain. Sometimes, she would start fights with me; she would throw the first punch. After the fight, she would always come up short; however, it would seem, she loved me more for it. I couldn't understand it.

One evening I told her, "Hey, I'm done with you. Dawanna it's time for you to kick rocks," a term meaning *get*. She started crying uncontrollably. To be totally honest, she lost her mind. She was trying to fight me; she just started throwing punches that I had to duck. Some were coming really quickly. I just wanted her to leave. I was tired of fighting with this girl and in a sense I felt for this girl because she had lost both her mother and her father at a young age.

How could you not feel for someone like this? She had also been raped as a kid and suffered emotionally from this. Even as an adult, often reflecting on that moment when she had no parents around. *I truly pray that God eases the suffering of her soul.*

At the time Big Harry was over. Harry weighed somewhere around 350 pounds and was six-foot-five.

"Hey, Harry," I said, "Can you take this girl somewhere?" He then said, "Not a problem, as long as I can drive your car?"

He talked to Dawanna for a minute. She then calmed down, and he took her somewhere, but that would not be the last I would see of Dawanna. One day Dawanna and I would have an experience that would defy all logic. Big Harry and I became good friends; however, it wouldn't start this way, at one point Big Harry wanted to kill me, or at least hurt me really badly. One thing I learned over the years is, you never mess with another man's property, unless you ask for permission.

Harry at the time was 20 years old and large. He always would come by with this young pretty dark chocolate girl named Shelley. Shelley had a body that was just in my mind, unbelievable. She was dark-skinned, short, lifted front and back, and she was about 105 in weight. She had a body that would make a married man not trust hisself alone with her.

How I met Shelley and Harry is kind of strange. They would come over and buy powder cocaine, a 20 here and a 40 there. Shelley would always be staring at me with those ebony eyes and later Harry would quit bringing her to the house. Well eventually, Shelley would make it to the house without Big Harry. She bought a 20, but to be honest I could have given it to her. Shelley started talking about Harry, after doing about three lines. She said "Harry is cool and everything, but his sword is so small." I said, "Excuse me?" She said, "His penis is so little."

I busted out laughing and then became very serious with my response. I'd wanted to see what she looked like without those blue jeans on for a long time now. "Shelley, I must assure you," I then said, "you won't be having that problem here." We had planned a date that weekend. She didn't know how much experience I had. I considered myself to be a true Trojan. At that time with the help of cocaine, I was going to give Shelley a night to remember. Without the cocaine, she had four serious hours and then a finisher in the morning. She just didn't know who she was messing with. Obviously, I didn't realize who I was messing with either. When she called that weekend, I couldn't believe it. She said, "I'm ready for you to pick me up, but Harry keeps calling, looking for me." I told her, "I will be right over, but meet me at the corner, down from the house." Big Harry was big, and a solid 350 plus. I knew he could hit hard; however, I just had to have Shelley. I then took her to Motel 6. At this point, I was really excited about seeing her. I was already on point, before she jumped into the car. I wanted her at this point, very badly. Basically, I just had to have my ass kicked.

Shelley had on some white pants that fit her as if they were painted on. I was thinking, *Girl, you will never forget this night. Man, I have wanted this for a long time.* As soon as we get in to the motel room, all clothes were off and we did some lines and we made passionate unlimited love, all night. I have to admit, I taught this youngster everything I knew. I also have to admit, I was scared as hell. Because of doing the drugs, paranoia had set in. I kept watching the shadows go by at the bottom of the door, thinking in my mind that one of those big shadows would be big Harry kicking the door down, even though he didn't know where we were. I just kept seeing him coming, inside my mind.

To keep from looking down at the shadows going by and worrying about Big Harry, I had to put a towel between the crack of the door and the floor and hope like hell he wasn't coming. In my mind, I could envision him kicking the door down. I still kept thinking he was coming; just the mere sight of him was intimidating.

We had sex in every way and position known to man. I worked Shelley out all that night without sleeping, and by morning time, I was still in stride. I never stopped, even while she was sleeping, because of the cocaine. I was again the man of steel. Again, I was Greedy D, didn't she know? I was a true Trojan and in my prime. She really didn't know who she was messing with. I was still trying to get mine. Once again, I didn't know who I was messing with either. Three days had nearly gone by at the motel and then I took her home. This was the first time she ever got broke off like that. I had turned her out. She didn't know that I was also one of the tag team champions from back east. I would one day let her experience my friend eagle. Just the simple up down sex, would never ever be appealing to her again. She would all ways remember for years to come, how I freaked her, even while in an intimate session with another, she would always remember that night, she would always remember the man of steel. From that day forward, Shelley was my freak; she would act like Stella and do what the fuck Greedy D would tell her. This would go on for another three weeks secretly without Big Harry knowing, or so I thought? She would still come over with Big Harry and it was hard to look at her, knowing if big Harry knew, he was going to be very unhappy, or should I say very pissed? When Big Harry found out for sure, what was going on with his woman, he wasn't happy, not at all.

You can tell when a brother hits hard, without his throwing a single punch. Just look at his hands. If they look big and like they have muscles on his fingers, you could be in for a long night, or a short one depending on where he decides to hit you.

When dealing with addiction, you also have to deal with why drugs and sex go hand and hand. "Fact," while talking to many addicts who tried fighting real hard at getting off of the drugs, one of the most common triggers for their relapse was the thought, or the idea, of having some female or male perform oral sex while they ingested the drug of their choice, at the same exact time. According to actual response, there is nothing more stimulating than this.

Big Harry finally had caught up with us when we had taken off for the weekend. Once again, I had taken her to a new sexual height. Big Harry, had finally caught on to our game plan, or should I say, our sexual endeavors.

This time when we pulled up in the cab at my sister's house, Big Harry was sitting in the front yard. He wasn't happy at all. First he started yelling at her saying, "What the fuck's up? What the fuck's up?" He then said to her, "How can you do me like that?" This nigga was crying and upset at the same time. Shelley and I had been having sex day and night, for three straight days, with no sleep. I was tired when I pulled up to my sister's house; I had no plans whatsoever to fight with Big Harry. It seemed like to me, as he yelled, he actually had gotten bigger and more intimidating. Whatever the case, I wasn't prepared for battle. I wanted sleep, relaxation, rest.

Nonetheless, this big brother then started yelling at me, "Hey nigga, bring your ass to the backyard." The only thing, I was thinking about was sleeping, not fighting this big brother. He just kept yelling at me, "Come on nigga," he said again, "Come on nigga." By this time Big Harry had already made it to the backyard. He was out there hitting the fence with his bare hands and knocking wood off it.

When I saw that, I was thinking *Damn. I'm fixing to get my first ass whipping that will be official.* That brother hit hard, at least it seemed that way, by the way the fence moved. At this age in life I knew that sometimes it's better to talk your way out of shit, especially if the odds are against you. I felt my pride would heal more quickly, than to have both headlights and front end taken out. Every time I added it up in my mind, I came up with the same answer; he's going to kick the Cowboy shit out of me. I would then say to myself, "Think fast Greedy, think fast Greedy."

I came up with some shit that, I had gotten from the movie *Scarface* and it actually worked. I also had a backup plan— you got to when dealing with something like this. I was too tired to be fighting Big Harry. All I wanted to do was sleep, whereas all Harry wanted was to kick my ass. On a day like this, if I hadn't been smart, he would have. There was nothing I could have done about it, at least on this day.

My sister had given me a knife, even she knew I was going to get a beating. I went into the backyard, when I said to him, "Harry, hey man, we can fight and you may or may not kick my ass, One thing is for sure, it won't be over because, I'm coming back nigga." I then said "Nigga, we are going to be killing each other and this girl Shelley is just going to be sucking on someone else." He started calming down and shaking his head "Right." I got him now, "Hey big Harry, I want you to start working for me." I said, "Aren't you tired of not ever having anything?"

I then said "Nigga, that will change if you start working for me." Big Harry and I would soon bond. Despite the indifferences, Harry accepted the fact that Shelley was mine now. He didn't like it still that I was sexing Shelley like crazy. He would later find out that I didn't mind if he still got him a taste from time to time and he did, after all, she started out with him. You got to let a freak be a freak.

He would later learn that, in the dope game, it doesn't really matter how you look. If, you are making money and you have the best dope, you can have any bitch, even if your sword is small like Big Harry's. Big Harry didn't get very many girls on his own at first and because he had sold a lot of drugs for me, I thought I would help him in that area. So I then gave Lucy some product for free to blow my man's brains out. A term for the ultimate rush, head. I will never forget, she was sucking his little thing, on the bed next to mine. She had the nigga hollering, it was his first time ever experiencing this. I was trying not to pay attention; however, I would look over and see her sucking on his little penis, when I couldn't help but to laugh out loud because, it was just a little head, no neck. Not that I was ever looking, but I had never seen anything like it before. Even the freak was telling him as she was bobbing up and down that it was small.

Big Harry and I would now start making serious paper. The money would flow, and Cowboy and I would work things out. I paid Cowboy off and I was back in his good graces. Cowboy liked the fact that whatever he gave me, he would get it back the next day, and this would put a smile on his face. Not only that, but I let him have my little freak Clarisse, from back in the hood. He had wanted Clarisse badly, for nearly three years. So I decided to let him have a taste. After Cowboy spent an hour with my freak, Cowboy was all good with me, he called me Cowboy again and started giving me kilos again, and all the weed I wanted.

CHAPTER 4

Making Money, Making Enemies

Search Warrant Signed

Cowboy had moved to Maryvale and our drug business flourished once again. I had never seen so much money and in many cases, we were making $10,000 per day. The bare minimum was $2,000.00. Back in 1986 this was good money by any standard. All we had to do was wake up and we were guaranteed to get paid. It was so good that, I had to move my soldier Greedy Bob in with me. We had a 24/7 business going. Back then, we had one Pager and each of us worked the pager in shifts of eight hours a piece.

This Pager went off day and night, every five minutes, every day, and we made sure no one would be left out. If you called this pager number, you could buy as much as a kilo or as little as a dime. In the beginning we didn't let anything get by.

Cowboy would come out to the house to pick up money twice in one day sometimes. He was all smiles. While our neighbors were having yard sales, just trying to make ends meet, we were having BBQ's and private parties at the house.

The Movie *Scarface* was always in the VCR, at all times. Shelley would soon introduce me to two more of her friends, Cianne and Glory. Me and Glory would hook up sexually. Once Shelley found out, she wasn't very understanding at all. She kept saying to me, how are you just going to sleep with my best friend, but it was her best friend who was just as guilty. Back in those days, it was all good.

So in retaliation, she gave Big Harry some, hell I didn't mind, I kind of liked the idea. Glory had more body than Shelley, and not only this, she was light-skinned. I would describe her skin as butter cream, butter pecan with green eyes, body measurements somewhere around 38-22-30, in my opinion. There was nothing fake about her. At this point in my life, we were like one big family and I was making so much money, plus I was now sexing Shelley, Glory, and I had another girl. She came around from time to time. I met her while riding around in my Greedy D, Pimp Mobile, she never had money, like I said, "I always had an alternative plan." In the Pimp Mobile, I picked up many girls, some didn't make it back to the house and most would earn a straight shot to the motel.

I sexed most female clients whom I sold drugs to, especially the fine ones. I couldn't wait for the time when one would call and wouldn't have any money. I always had an alternative plan for them, back in these days. I didn't have color barriers—I wanted them all.

Remember I was Greedy D. I had a Mini Blazer that had too much chrome and Dayton's wire rims that just came out. I also had the humps, the loud music that would make you want to call the police, if I drove through your apartment complex and trust me some did. I had it lowered and also had painted in pinstripe and chrome the name Greedy D.

I was a fool; I was running around in this vehicle which stood out like a sore thumb, thinking everything was just fine, it wasn't. Once again, the drugs were starting to take total control of me and everyone in the house. Once again I was starting to lose my fucking mind. I had at least 15 different weapons in the house; I also was starting to get paranoid.

We were starting out our mornings early, using cocaine. All of our thoughts seemed rational; however, I can tell you now that, nothing was rational. We would each do somewhere around a tablespoon of coke each morning we woke up, just Harry, Bob and I. We would then powder our nose, once every hour to maintain our high.

Bob was smart he would do less. More and more each day Harry and I would do as much as we could. Altogether at this point, we were probably doing somewhere around a half ounce a day. If any girls were around, we would ration out theirs. Greedy Bob kept telling me, "Hey Greedy D, something just isn't right man, it seems that the police were everywhere I made money today." Big Harry also verified that he too, was starting to see more cops on his runs also. I kept giving them more and more cocaine explaining to them that, if the cops came here, we were going to shoot it out with them. Greedy Bob was saying "Yeah, we will shoot it out." He was just kidding, but I was serious.

I went and got one of the guns while displaying it openly and saying that they better not come here. I'm ready. Part of my arsenal was a Mini 14, an uzi assault rifle, several sawed off shotguns, a 45, two 9mm's and a 357 magnum, along with a Mack 10. We even had several Deer rifles and a 30-30, we had enough fire power to keep them at bay or so we thought.

One thing for sure about all of this was the police were coming. We just didn't know which day, and no one would get a chance to reach for a gun. Little did I know, the police were trying to make a buy of cocaine from my house. Who they would send would surprise me and everyone that knew him. He's the only one that was close enough to bring my organization to its knees. At that time we didn't sell to people we didn't know, this made it hard for them to just come in. However, when they came, they would leave no stone unturned.

Everyone would go to jail, including the dogs. They shot one of the dogs in the head barely grazing him. That pit bull took off running and hasn't been seen to this day. They also came with bigger guns, and they weren't happy. The way they took me out, would take three years for me to realize who actually did this to me. When I found out, we were both in the county jail, but a big steel door separated us when I had said to him, "I want your blood." I have not seen him since. Rolo went to North high school with me; he also came to my mother's house before this one.

The girls liked him at North high school. Back in high school, he was always with at least two girls. He carried his boom box with him all over campus, playing the latest tunes. He was very intelligent and good-looking to all the women. He would later become one of the best DJ's for afterhours parties because of his ability to scratch on the turntables. I used to let him bring different freaks over to the house to get his freak on.

He was the only one who could've helped the police bring me down, but back then, as close as he was to me, I just didn't want to believe it. However, the destroyer had gotten to him, as it had gotten to me and nothing was off limits. We probably didn't see Rolo for four months.

One day he started showing up again, but this time he would always come over with guys whom we didn't know. They would always be white guys who would never come in. The reason why we hadn't been seeing him is because he had violated probation and was waiting to get his snitch card. They never came in the house meaning, the undercover cops always came in cars with very dark, tinted windows that were difficult to see in. After seeing for the first time who was bringing him over, he was warned. We would say to him, "Hey Rolo man, don't be bringing these people over here man." He would say "D, you know I'm cool." Rolo was very intelligent and sometimes, a little too intelligent for his own good. I was out of cocaine; however, I was expecting Cowboy to come through soon with my issue. I was assuming that the police had already made their first buy through Rolo because they had a search warrant signed. The date was for one week.

That meant there were seven days for the Police to make their move. There was only one problem with this. Rolo had informed them that I didn't have any more dope. So they were waiting for Cowboy to bring the dope; they just didn't know who Cowboy was. Six days had gone by and the police were getting a little impatient, they wanted action, they wanted me.

March 10, 1987, about 4 a.m. The cops were coming and hell was coming with them.

Finally I had gotten the call I was waiting for. Cowboy said to me on the phone, "Hey, Cowboy, I got something for you, come on by." Once I had gotten there, we talked. It had been 10 long days, since I had had some cocaine. He then said to me, once I had gotten there, "This is all I have, take this for now and I will get you some more before you run out."

Needless to say, I was excited that I was back in business, at least I thought I was. I remember picking up the dope from Cowboy, going by my freak Lucy's house and getting my head blown, and then going back to my house. The whole trip didn't take more then an hour and a half. Once I had gotten home, I looked across the street and saw a white van, this was a vehicle that I had never seen parked directly across the street before. I thought that this was strange, but I was high and I couldn't wait to get in the house to get my freak on, after all, I had a lot of energy with me, about a half-pound worth.

Ten minutes had gone by and there was a knock at the door. It was Rolo and for the first time ever, Rolo had a half-pound of cocaine with him. This was strange because at this time, I was Rolo's connection and now he was trying to be mine and front me some dope? His exact words were, "I know you are still out D and that's why I brought you some dope." He then pulled out what the police had given to him to give to me, so that they could raid my house. The police were already outside at this point waiting on Rolo to give me the dope. They didn't know that, I had already got some dope from Cowboy because they didn't have a wiretap, and I hadn't seen Rolo in a couple of days, nor had I talked to him on the phone.

They had to raid me that morning because their search warrant was about to expire and not only this, they had gathered up a huge force outside so, the drugs had to be in the house. I didn't know any of this at the time, however. I explained to Rolo, "I just saw Cowboy and he just took care of me." I then showed Rolo what I had and said to him, "I think this is a lot better than what you got?" He then snorted a line of my dope, to verify that it indeed was cocaine. He then immediately left; no more communication.

Ten minutes after the informant left, all hell would break loose

The ATF, Glendale Special Tactical Unit, along with the Maryvale Street Crimes Unit and the Phoenix Police Department all raided my house. They closed the whole neighborhood down; you couldn't get in or out. From afar, it looked like a police convention. It seemed as if at least 100 police officers participated. They rushed in with Army fatigues on, and it looked to me as if they had M-16's with the infrareds. That's all I could see, when they kicked my bedroom door open that hit me in the face, while I was buck naked. All I could see was the little dots all over me, as they pointed their weapons at my head and chest. I knew at this time that they meant business as they yelled out commands, "Get the fuck down right now, or we will blow your fucking head off." I still had cocaine residue on my nose when I did exactly what they told me to do.

All the shooting it out that we had planned proved to be for nothing. We never got a chance to get to a gun. With the overwhelming display of force, they took down my operation within 20 minutes. As a matter of fact, once they had us all stabilized and ready to take us out and put us in to the police vans, the neighbors gathered outside and were clapping their hands and yelling, good job officers. I yelled back, "When I get out, I'm going to kill all you motherfuckers. The very next day, we were all released; no neighbors came outside at all. It would be that way until I would move out of the neighborhood, one month later. Rolo was always pretty smart, maybe a little smarter than me. He came over that next day and said to me, "Hey, I heard you had got busted yesterday." He was smart because, if he didn't come by, I would have suspected him. He played me like a fiddle. Any time you get raided at your place of business, it's usually that last smiling face that did you in—I just didn't want to believe it.

As Mom has always said to me, "Son, what's in the dark, will always come to the light." She would have no idea that, this great saying would also play a role in her life. Once again, this would be proven. Not only did they take my dope, they also took all my money. I would also have a court date. Shortly after the raid, I would get my first court date and look at all the items that they had seized. I would realize that, they didn't turn in all the drugs which were taken out of my house, to their superiors. They had listed on record that I had only a small baggy of Marijuana. I had a lot more than that. Somewhere around a half-pound, which is visibly different than a small baggy. What fool would stand up in court and say, "By the way, your Honor, I had more weed than that."

I was at this time considered a fool; however, I wasn't that foolish. Some cops are dirty too and some like to get high too. I would meet a bunch of crooked police, in the prison system. I just couldn't understand how they could just come in and get my dope, after being out for 10 straight days. I kept saying to myself, "How could they know when to come in and get it?"

In the beginning, I had thought it was Lucy who did me; after all, she knew I just had scored. It wasn't her. I wouldn't find out for sure, until three years later. When I did find out, I would want his blood and he knew he could never look in my face again. Once again, however, I was back on my feet shortly after the raid. I was big balling one month prior. Once again, on foot. Once again, I was doing my own product and the nosebleeds would continue to get worse.

Bob and Big Harry would eventually go in their own direction, after all we were broke now and Cowboy wanted to get paid for the half-pound that he had just given us. No exceptions. I tried to explain to Cowboy saying, "How can you expect me to pay for this, when I'm already paying, because I got a case now." I then said to him, "I'm not dragging you into it." I said to him, "I'm taking care of this like a man." Cowboy still had no understanding whatsoever. He wanted his money and now. My court case came up, so I hired one of the best lawyers for drug laws to represent me. He worked it out with the State that I would do 45 days in the Department of Corrections and then do intake at The Arizona Family Drug Rehabilitation Center for a two-year program, while on seven years probation. I couldn't believe I actually signed this; however, I didn't want to go back to prison. I agreed to this shit, while knowing in the back of my mind that, I couldn't make seven years of probation. Trying to make two years would prove to be difficult. I didn't want to believe it, but going back to prison would be my destiny.

Cowboy and I would be at odds with each other, once again. I just couldn't see paying him when I was the one that was going to prison for this shit. He knew that they had taken all the money and the drugs I had around the house. Once again, I had lost all I had. Either it had been taken in the raid, or I had traded it for the dope after the raid, or I just simply couldn't live the finer side of life in my mind. At this point, I had been living with my girlfriend. To top it all off, I was on foot and taking the money that my girlfriend got once a month from the government and fucking it off, with other freaks.

I was tripping. I started selling tens and twenties out of her house when one night I noticed that the Police had set up surveillance on the apartment we were living in. So what I did was I would wait till the next night, when they would come back. These were undercover cops and the way they had their surveillance set up, they had a direct view of my door and they could see who came in and out. So what I did, I walked out my door and then I stood there for a minute. They didn't know it, but I now had them under counter-surveillance. I then looked over to my left and then walked in that direction. After walking for a few minutes to get out of their view, I then took off running, to get behind them. What I did was, I sneaked up behind them. There were about three hippy-looking, white undercover cops, standing right by their truck wondering, where I had gone? If they were black cops, I would not have noticed them. But these guys stood out to me. So I then approached their truck when they looked up in disbelief. That's when I said to them, "Hey, what's up?" The three of them immediately jumped in their truck and took off. Their cover was blown.

I would then meet Chow, he was Mexican and he would later become my blood brother and nothing has changed to this day. He had just moved here from Midland, Texas. He came here with wife, kids, a couple of sisters and a couple of brothers. He is a hard worker, and he had a fine wife. We would start chopping it up, a term meaning speaking. Somehow or another, we had started talking about cars. I then said to him, "I got a Mini Blazer, just pimped out to the max," and I started to describe it in detail. He then stopped me in the middle of the conversation and said "Hey, I remember that truck! It was at the motel for a few days, when I first moved here from Midland, Texas." I then asked him, "What motel are you referring to?" He then said, "Motel 6, 27th Ave and Indian School Road." I then said to him, "Don't ever mention this when I'm around my girl, because at the time, I was with another freak." He said, "Okay but man, that's a bad truck." Motel 6 was my hangout back in those days. I spent a lot of money and time there.

Here is where I would be humiliated by the Phoenix Police Department to the max. This would be even more humiliating, than anything to me. I was a bad influence on Chow because he was a married man. I would keep him out late sometimes; however, he would always go home to his fine wife. He always respected her. This night would be no different for him, but strange as fuck for me and very, very humiliating.

I remember snorting some powder rocks, while he was driving me around when I looked up, with powder residue still on my nose, and saw this freak walking down the street. I then said "Dog stop, I want to pick her up." I then said to her "Do you do cocaine?" she then said "Hell, yeah." As her eyes popped open real wide. I then said to her, "Come on with me, so we can party." She then jumped in the truck that Chow was driving and sat on my lap. I said, "Yeah, baby, we are going to have some fun, F-U-N." I would indeed have some fun in the beginning; however, in the end, this smile would be wiped off of my face.

Chow then hit the gas, so he could get me and this freak to the motel quickly, as I had suggested. As soon as she jumped on my lap, I immediately had my hands on her breast, when I felt a very sharp ice pick in her hands, as I was reaching for them. I then asked her, "What's that for?" she then said, "It's for protection." I didn't know it at the time but, she had some serious mental issues.

Well, Chow dropped us off and then went home. She already had a room at the Motel 6, one of my favorite spots at the time. Soon as we got in the door, by this time, you already know by now what happened. Once again, I was the man of steel and I put serious work in on her. By early that morning, she was trying to get some rest, but I was still trying to get mine.

I remember going to the bathroom and when I came out she was on the phone with somebody. She said, "They want to talk to you." I said, "They, who wants to talk to me?" I then said to her, "But nobody knows I'm here." She then handed me the phone. The voice on the phone said, "Come outside right now." Then I heard the dial tone. I said to her, "Who in the fuck is that?" I peeked through the curtain. She wouldn't tell me who it was; she just looked at me strangely and kind of crazily. I was still buck naked and on point when I looked through the window and saw a Clint Eastwood, pointed directly at the window It was aimed directly at my head. There was a cop on the other end, of what appeared to be a 44 Magnum, one of the most powerful handguns in the world. He then started giving me commands; he yelled at me, "Open up the door now. You are under arrest."

I had just come out the bathroom, still high from the cocaine we had just done, before I went in. When this cop put the Clint Eastwood in my face and I saw the many other cops waiting to greet me once the door was opened, I wasn't high anymore.

Now I was naked and not on point anymore either. To make matters even worse, it was around 10 a.m. on that Saturday morning, when all the motel guests were out of their rooms watching all the commotion going on outside. I then opened the door and all guns were drawn down on me. The cops would then snatch me out of the room with no clothes on; everybody was looking at me. My eyes were all big and shit, from the drugs I had just done. They had me lying face down on the sidewalk, with my butt cheeks flapping in the air, for everyone to see. This was humiliating for me. However; they were calling all the shots and I had to obey. I was still wondering at this time, what the fuck did I do to deserve this? I would then find out that this girl, while I was in the bathroom had made a call to the police department saying that, I had kidnapped her and I was holding her hostage in one of the rooms.

I'm glad someone on the force had the common sense to investigate the matter a little further. We had empty cocaine baggies all over the room and empty alcohol bottles. The room was rented in her name as well. It didn't look like the scene of someone being held against her will. While sitting in the police car, handcuffed and still naked. One of them brought my clothes to me and took off the cuffs, so I could then put them on. They then said to me after holding me there for awhile, why they did me like they did me and they thought she was crazy. They never apologized for the humiliation that they caused me and just allowed me to leave. I was on foot when, I walked over to the nearby 7-Eleven and called for someone to pick me up. While thinking to myself, *This is real messed up*. However, this wouldn't deter me from picking up other women. *You have to pay for everything you do in life: I was just paying more dues.*

Two weeks had gone by and it was time for the police to raid our apartment. I knew that they were still watching me. I just didn't know how they were going about it. So what I did was I came up with some plaster, which was in powder form. It looked just like cocaine. I put it in a big plastic bag. It really looked like the real thing. We then left the house for a few days. This is when the Phoenix Police Dept would come in and I know they thought they found the mother lode, when they saw the plaster. They had to leave the apartment empty-handed though. I guess this was my way of getting back at them for treating me this way at the motel.

CHAPTER 5

Lockdown

Forced Drug Rehabilitation

Somewhere Around
January of 1988

I entered the Department of Corrections for 45 days as stipulated by my probation agreement.

The very first day I got there, these Aryan motherfuckers didn't have anything better to do than to fuck with me. They kept hollering, "Fresh meat!" from a distance yelling, "Hey, fish!" I then would yell back, "Come fuck with me." They never would take it any farther than that, they didn't know at the time that I wasn't the one. I wasn't a punk. I knew just what to do, so the whole time I was there at Fort Grant Prison, I stayed on the weight pile and hung out with my brothers. Immediately following my incarceration of 45 days, I would sign up for intake, into the Arizona Family Drug Rehabilitation Center. By this time, I had lost everything that I had made from selling cocaine again.

Often while walking the pavement, I would say to myself, "How in the hell did I let myself get to this point again?"

Man, I couldn't believe it. There I was making big money and now I hadn't got a dime so to speak and I was walking once again. They say, easy comes, easy goes; this would be proven in this case. They also say, what goes up, must come down. This was the second time I had had a lot and once again it was all gone. To top it all off, I was broke and my truck was repossessed. I started buying cocaine from other dealers. I didn't have any pull any more on the streets. It got worse, every little bit of dope I would get, I would do it all, instead of making money with it.

It had gotten to the point that, I wouldn't even sell any to people who were calling. I would just tell them when they called that "I just ran out," while looking down at my sack and taking a cocaine rock and pushing it up into my nose and snorting it. By this time I had overdosed at least three more times and on the last trip to the hospital, the doctor said I had damaged my heart. I had then started doing outpatient, over at Terro's Drug Treatment Center. At the same time, right around this time, I was doing more meth. Shelley didn't like me high on meth because, she knew with this stuff, I would be the man of steel, long after I ran out and she wouldn't get any sleep during these episodes. We began to have more arguments because of the amounts I was doing. I would just tell her, "You don't tell me what the fuck to do, you here."

They had me on depression medication over at Terro's Drug Out Patient Clinic. Basically I was losing my mind again and I was depressed and stressed out to the max. Just about every day would start out with cocaine or meth and end with it. I couldn't control this shit, no matter how much I would tell myself that I could. I used to tell myself that "I was just going to do a twenty and quit." I was a fool for ever thinking that one. This would lead sometimes to going on a four-day mission. Even worse, I would one day go to the motel with this girl who left, as soon as I ran out of the drug. I sat there depressed and out of my fucking mind because, my girlfriend was looking for me and once again, I had tricked off all my money with these hoes.

Once again, I was depressed to the maximum. I took out my gun from my pants; I was tired of this shit. I wanted this shit to end. I was in tears, sitting there with the gun pointed to my head. "I'm sick of this, I'm sick of this shit."

This is all I could say, "I'm sick of this, I'm so tired of this fucking shit." Is what kept flashing through my mind. I sat there alone thinking, "Why can't I stop this shit." At this point, I had tried so many times unsuccessfully to quit and nothing at this point was helping me. For some reason, I just couldn't pull the trigger, once again, I called out to the Lord. I also called my girlfriend; she didn't know that I had the gun aimed at my head. I told her that, "I am so depressed again and I have fucked off the money, again." She felt for me and came and got me from the motel. That's when she noticed I had a gun. She also wanted to tell me, she thought she might be pregnant. This was when I told her, "I was real close to ending it all." I had taken this woman through pure hell.

When going through these different emotions, while using hard drugs, the family bond is the first to be harmed. In most cases, it take years to be fully repaired and in many cases, it's totally destroyed.

This wasn't the real me, this is what I had become, after becoming addicted to cocaine. The real me was hard to see, because my life had become so ugly. It was hard to see what I could have been, if given the opportunity. The God whom I wasn't serving, would pour out more of his blessing upon me. My Daughter, Raven, would be born on of all days, Father's Day. I was at the lowest point in my life and I was in a drug rehabilitation center at the time. He would show mercy and love for me, although I wasn't worthy of receiving it.

I honestly felt that if I went to this treatment center, I would give it a sincere chance. I would try to honestly kick this thing. This monkey cocaine and meth that was riding on my back, so to speak, would prove harder to kick than I could have ever imagined.

I remember being so high one night, and I just started crying and couldn't stop. I remember walking into Pilgrim Rest Baptist Church, this was my old church, I had nowhere else to go, my girlfriend, whom I was now living with, told me that morning not to return because, I had taken her $200 and bought dope with it. I had tried to make money with it; however, I failed in the process because, I messed it off with a freak.

God's Servant Would Intervene, Reverend Alexis Thomas from Pilgrim Rest Baptist Church

Later on that day, after running out of drugs, major depression had taken shape. I tried calling my girlfriend and trying to beg her for forgiveness, but at this time, she herself couldn't take it anymore. She was tired.

I remember walking one night, on the east side of town crying, not having anywhere to go. At this time, I had burnt all bridges and I had turned my family against me, or so I thought. I was saying over and over in my mind, *Why can't I beat this? Why can't I beat this?* The tears would start pouring down my chest heavily when I looked up and there was the church that I had grown up going to. I was broke and in despair—I also smelled bad. I was hurting inside something fierce. I was hopeless and helpless; I was for sure mentally destroyed. *Why can't I beat this?* This thought wouldn't leave my mind.

Pilgrim Rest Baptist Church

It was Sunday night and I will never forget it. I didn't know if the church was open, but I turned the handle of the door and it was open. *All glory and praise to God.*

I walked in and there was one woman there, who looked like a secretary of the church or something. I immediately sat in the back pews crying out loud and I couldn't stop. I couldn't help but think about the lifestyle that I had been living. I kept saying in my mind over and over again, *Why can't I stop using these drugs, why can't I stop?*

Reverend Alexis Thomas

As I repeated this in my mind, the tears kept falling from my eyes, soaking my shirt, when the lady in the church, came up to me asking, "Sir, are you okay?" I repeated, "no," very softly, and then said, "I must talk to your Pastor." I couldn't stop crying when she immediately went to the phone and called Pastor Alexis Thomas, a true man of God, not knowing if he was busy, or even if he had the time. This pastor would make time.

This fine man of God, this fine young Pastor, stopped whatever he was doing that night. *"All glory to God."* He came into the church and approached me, asking, "What's wrong?" I said to him with tears still visibly rolling down my face, "I've been doing cocaine, and I just can't stop. Plus, I stole my girlfriend's rent money and messed it off and now she doesn't want to see me anymore." Pastor Thomas knew exactly what to do. He then said to me, "We are going to pray." *"All glory to God. Thank you, Jesus."* After praying for me, I couldn't cry anymore.

He then called my girlfriend that night and after identi-
fying who he was and asking her could I come back home
and could she forgive me for what I had done, she then agreed.
Pastor Thomas took me all the way to Maryville to her apartment. Pastor Thomas, a true man of God, from my heart,
thank you. To this day, I could never say I'm sorry enough
to this woman. I didn't know it, but the God that this young
Pastor prayed to and the God that my mother had continu-
ously reminded me about was indeed listening.

My mom had told me as a kid that, she took my name
out of the Bible because it was good. As I looked at myself
and my life back then and at that particular time, what I saw
was all bad. This could be construed as being evil.

Little did I know that, it would get even worse, before it would get better

Nothing could have ever prepared me for what was to come
next. It was time to seriously kick this thing. Looking back
on my life, it was a total disaster. I'm directly responsible for
the suffering of so many. I had to at least try. I would later
find out that, it would take more than I could have ever imagined to beat this thing. The problem was, I liked the way it
tasted; I liked the way it drained once I snorted it, even worse,
I dreamed about it. Sometimes, I would wake from a dream
craving it and at this point, I would have to have it. To add to
these difficulties in mind, I had to have this before, during and
after sex. This would prove to be one of the hardest things to
ever to deal with in my life. I needed help with this sexual

addiction, which would go untreated, so in a sense I was destined to fail. At this time in my life, failure was an option.

Unbeknownst to me, my mother kept praying for me. She did not, as she had promised, ever give up on me. This is my example of what you call a mother. God would later show favor towards this woman.

March of 1988

I had not been at the Arizona Family Drug Rehabilitation and Treatment Center long when I realized that I would not make it in there. My first day, I wanted to jump on one of these other addicts. These people actually got kicks out of fucking with you every day and the way they got you to remain there was the threat of going back to prison. My sentence was seven years. For the first time in a while, I had been off cocaine and it made me feel good. This place was coed and I didn't like it. However; they had only three rules. No sex, no drugs, no fighting. They left out a few things; however, they had a bunch of little ones. It wasn't long before I was chalking my name up on the board for stupid stuff like, walking on the grass. When you were asked to chalk it up, that meant you lost your visits. Needless to say I lost my visits a lot.

My probation officer would get a call that next morning and every month, for the duration that I was there, telling her that I wanted out of that place. Her answer never changed each time. She said "David, there is nowhere else for you to go but prison." Each time, I would hang up the phone, with no other further request.

These people at the center kept you depressed; they did this by fucking with you constantly. They considered me a character. So this was my help that I received during my group meeting. This is the only meeting that a personal counselor would sit in on. This is what I had to say daily and indefinitely and nightly in general meetings. "Hi, my name is David and I'm a dope fiend and I'm still showing dope fiend behaviors. How may I help you?" We had fifty plus clients in this place and it seemed like everyone wanted to play. Before I could say anything, I had to say this preface statement.

After saying that statement over one hundred times in one day, one could get a little upset. Then you have these older family members going around playing police hollering, David you need to be redundant, when I forgot to say the preface statement. Then from there, I had to go report to my counselor, who then said, "Go chalk it up on the board." Then you get no visits for that week and sometimes the next. Sometimes for up to two months, depending on the violations.

Just about every week, I was losing my visit, until I learned how to play the game. It was the treatment center's belief that they should keep you stressed out and that's when you would display your dope fiend behaviors and that's when they would treat you. Their idea was to break you all the way down and then rebuild you. The only problem was they left a couple major items out of my treatment. I was addicted to sex, as well as to the life style of selling drugs. I liked selling drugs. They gave no treatment for this nor had any answers, so I was destined for failure. They wanted you to snitch on your friends and this was always hard for me to do. You either learned to practice the game, or you would fail and go back to prison, even worse, go back to getting high. These were the thoughts of the counselors. So, I thought I would practice telling, or positive growth, as they would call it.

They had broken me down after six months and now even worse, I was a Snitch. I caught Jock sneaking some coffee into the center. Jock was an older family member; I was considered a younger family member. Coffee was considered a drug inside this place and I had caught Jock bringing them in. While in general meeting, I stood Jock up saying, "This is a confrontation, Jock, would you please stand up? Jock, I caught you sneaking coffee in yesterday. Jock you need to be held responsible by your counselor for violating rules and regulations for bringing coffee into the institution."

Jock then looked over at the counselor who told him to go outside to the board and chalk it up. Jock then looked at me with those eyes that seemed to say, "Nigger, have you lost your fucking mind, you don't fuck with me."

Jock lost his visit that weekend and received a preface statement, similar to the one I had for doing so. "Hi, my name is Jock and I'm a dope fiend and I'm still showing dope fiend behaviors. How may I help you?" After the meeting, everyone congratulated me for snitching on Jock. To me I felt like a fucking asshole because, they had finally broken me down and had me doing something that I was totally against. Like I said, they considered me to be a character, so they thought they would help to stop me from acting foolish. So they ordered me to act a fool every night, for 60 seconds in general meeting, daily and indefinitely with no restriction. They should not have done this.

The first night for my help, I came into the meeting with shades on and my boom box. I instructed the leader of general meeting to put on the clock, for sixty seconds. Once he said go, I played some music and danced for sixty seconds with these shades on. I looked real foolish bumping the music and being the only one dancing in the meeting, while everyone was sitting down watching in amazement. This was my help and this is what they wanted me to do, to help me.

They wanted to see a fool and unknowing to me and the counselors, this fool would eventually show up. Well after the fifth day of doing this, I was getting tired and running out of stuff to do. One day while I was making an early morning raid on the walk-in freezer, looking for food to steal for my room, I found a long, strong, 12 inches of hard sausage. I started waving it around, when I came up with an idea for my help in general meeting. That night while in the meeting again, I instructed the leader to put me on, so I could do what I was told. I then started saying to the family members, "I have help to act absurd, daily and indefinitely and nightly in general meetings with no restrictions."

The Family Member, who was running the meeting at the time was looking for his signal from me. He was then looking at his watch; once he got the signal he said, "Go." I then started saying to one of the girls, "Hey baby, could you tell me what this is?" while, reaching towards my zipper on my pants. This girl was a former hoe, who was in there for rehab, for hoeing and drugs, I then slowly zipped down my pants, while telling her, "Can you tell me what this is?" Once again, people were looking around, eyebrows standing up straight and saying quietly, "I know he isn't going to do that." It probably took me all of 10 seconds to reach in my pants and pull the long, hard, sausage out.

I had my coat on at the time, so when I pulled the sausage out, every body thought I pulled the real one out and then, I started flapping it up and down like it was the real one and everyone in the meeting was laughing so hard except for this girl, who was now crying and the counselor, who didn't look happy at all either. It was during this time that, I knew by the appearance of this counselor's face that I would lose my visits again.

She would then tell me immediately after the meeting, "Go chalk it up on the board." I later apologized to the girl.

I would lose my visits again. I explained that this is what they wanted me to do, to act absurd, in general meeting. She said, "You have taken it too far." Jock had not forgotten about me making him lose his visits and look bad amongst his peers, so Jock was watching me for a long time. I just didn't know it, with my too smart ass. Jock wanted some "James Brown," some "Payback" and soon he would get his chance. Jock told me one day in general meeting when I least expected it, "David would you stand up please. This is a confrontation." At that particular time, I was doing so much wrong, I knew I was in violation of something, as he stood me up to point out my wrongs. David he said, "The other day, I caught you sneaking your boom box into your room. David." he said, "You need to be reprimanded for violation of rules and procedures. See your counselor after the meeting."

Once again I had lost my visits, "Damn." Nearly a year had gone by and I was really feeling like what they had taught me would help me. I had been clean for nearly a year when I was asked, would I help one of the guys out,when he went to the dentist. They would seldom let you go anywhere by yourself so, they would send a snitch with you, they called it support. So in this case I was the snitch. Once we had made it to the dentist's office, we then went up the street, over to this girl's house, which this guy knew. Before we could get there for some reason, the counselor had doubled back after dropping us off and found out we had left.

This was a major violation. Well, once we had gotten back, they told me at the dentist's office that the Arizona Family Drug Treatment Center wanted me to call. I called them about four hours after they dropped us off. They straight up told me that they didn't want me back; however,

Bob could come back. I was scared at that point because, this is a two-year program and I'd only been there for a year. My P.O. could violate me and send me back to prison, for not completing the program. I called my girlfriend and told her I had got kicked out of the program and that I would be going over to my mom's.

The very next day, I then called my P.O. and explained what had happened and then begged her to at least to give me a chance to prove myself, since I had been clean for over a year now. She was hesitant when she agreed, but also warned me that if I messed up, I would surely return to prison. I then said to her, "You have nothing to be concerned about, that I won't be going back to prison because, I am a changed man." My P.O. was mean and strict, she had to be because, she knew exactly what and who she was dealing with, there was no doubt about this. *I was a hardened criminal, who would sell crack to my family members—no one was exempt.*

So after being on probation for awhile, l hatched up a plan to get rid of her—I just moved to another area. This way, they would have to change my probation officer. My mom and I moved to another area, without her knowing my reason for wanting to do so. However, I never really stayed with my mom; actually, I lived with my girlfriend and our daughters. The new P.O didn't know this.

In order for probation to really work, when the probationers move, they must keep that same probationary officer. She or he alone is better equipped to deal with a monster like myself. They can be more like Johnny on the spot to deal with issues that get out of hand.

Inadvertently, This Is How the Destroyer Would Be Able to Sneak Back In

I figured that if my address remained at my mother's house, then they could never come looking for me at my girlfriend's house. They gave me another P.O named Jesse, who was different from the P.O. before. Jesse explained to me that day that he would not violate me. He said that, I was going to do that to myself. He then said that the only thing he would do is provide the rope in which to hang me. He shot straight from the hip and he would keep his promise.

Once again I repeated this, saying: "I'm a changed man, Jesse." I also informed him that I was going to school now and trying to make something serious of my life. I remember just a week prior, signing up for Lambson Business College and being accepted. I had been free of alcohol and drugs for over a year and a half but, buy the time I started my first day of college, I had already smoked my first joint and drank my first beer.

To make things even worse, I had already bought my first little sack of cocaine, so I could make some extra money to get me by. This was one of the biggest mistakes I could ever have done. I figured that since I had been away from it for awhile, that I had build up a defense for it. I was only fooling myself when I thought this. Not only this, but the devil was sending one of his servants to greet me. His name was Sonny; I had met him through Peanut, who would later take a shotgun blast to his dome—yes, dead on arrival.

This was very sad for me because, he was such a young man who had a lot of promise and a lot of potential and may the Lord God have mercy on his soul. Unlike me, the destroyer was successful at destroying this man's life. When I had gotten the news, as well as everybody else, I was in total disbelief that he would take his own life. *Just like me, he couldn't kick this habit, unlike me he had given up.*

CHAPTER 6

The Devil's Servant

Sonny, I have to admit, was one of the coldest white boys I had ever met. No matter where he went, drama followed. This guy carried fake kilos with him and fake stacks of money with him. This is what he did every day, all day, for a living. He was built like Snoop Dogg, so he would always wear long-sleeve shirts. I could tell he had a little man complex and this is only one of the reasons, he carried his pistol daily. He also had fine sisters with him, different ones almost every single time and they all were fine, no Mud Ducks.

This white boy I have to admit was bad, in every sense of the word. I was trying to buy a little sack and that's when "Peanut" gave us the introduction. Sonny told me one night, "D, he said, you are making money the hard way, let me show you how to really make some money." It's very seldom that a white man could school a black man on drama, however he would do this. He would prove to be a professional.

Sonny said, "D, I make and spend money the way I do because, I don't have to pay someone for the dope I get." He then said that, "there's nothing like free money, D." To give you an example he said, "Come with me tonight, and I will show you, nigger." Also, I wasn't accustomed to a white man calling me nigger at this point in my life; however, he was try-ing to pay me, so I went along with it for awhile. Sonny picked me up that night when I said to him, "Where are we going, man?" He then said, "It's just a weed deal, Greedy, it won't take long It's out in Scottsdale, Arizona." On the way, Sonny stopped at the store and bought some big tall trash bags.

He then later on down the street, stopped on the side of road and said, "Greedy, pull up some of those weeds." I said, "Serious?" He said, "Nigger, I'm going to show you how to make some free money." He then got on the phone and dialed this guy's number, who was expecting him to call about the weed. Sonny told him, "Hey man, I'm about 10 minutes away and you better have all the fucking money." This guy on the phone said, "I got the money however; I would like to see it." Sonny then went the fuck off when he said, "Motherfucker, you going to question my integrity, when I drove all the way out here, motherfucker?" He then said, "We are going to do it my way, I don't fucking know you." By the time Sonny got through yelling at this guy, he was more than willing to do the deal. We drove up that evening, Sonny lowered the window on my side, the guy then said to Sonny, "Is this some good stuff?" Sonny then replied "Oh yeah," he then threw Sonny the money, I then gave the guy the big bag of oleanders, we then drove off. *These type of Jacks always require an inside man.*

The whole deal didn't take more than two hours to complete. Sonny boasted on the way home, while counting his money. He then said, "See, D, see how easy that was?" I said, "Yeah, man." He then threw me $200 for going. I then said to him, "Man, I liked that." I also said to him, "The only thing I did was put the oleanders in the bag and I got paid $200 for it." Sonny explained, "Always, get people around other people when doing your Jack Move and most will not check the product." He then said, "Always try to keep them off balance."

He also said that "I make thousands nearly every day, Greedy, from doing this." I believed him because he was flashing the Rollie and he dressed nice everyday and drove nice cars. I couldn't wait to do my first Jack Move with Sonny and to make things even better for my first time out, Sonny was willing to assist. Sonny would then say that sometimes he sees the guys he jacks and most don't do anything over time. Sonny never explained the pitfalls from living this type of lifestyle.

But some people don't forget, especially after losing $25,000 at one time. He said as long as you keep it to a kilo at a time, they usually get over it at one point. This was bullshit, but at this time Sonny was making a lot of sense to me.

Greedy D's Second Jack Move

Sonny also left out another big part; you have to be great at acting. Well, I always wanted to be an actor, but would I be good enough to fool some very upset motherfuckers? This would soon be the question time was going to tell. After all, my life stood in the balance, in many of the cases. Shit, when my life was on the line, I would prove to be at least an Academy Award contender. I started buying small sacks from these Mexicans I had just met. Now it was time to put Sonny's plan into progress. I told these guys I knew a guy who wanted to buy a kilo. They were excited when they gave me a price that was real high, when I agreed.

I would have agreed to any price. They couldn't wait to make the sale, so we played with their minds for a few minutes, to increase the desire to make the sale. I told them that my guy was afraid because he didn't know them, so all he wanted to do was drop the money off and pick up the stuff and leave. I said he didn't want to see anyone. They didn't know it but, by evening's fall, they would be short. I told them, "This guy is really afraid because, he already had some problems with the cops before and he doesn't want to see anyone." These guys would be okay with this because, they didn't want to see anyone either; they bought into the drama. So far the move was working, just as planned.

These guys were so into the profit that they were going to make after the sale that, they forgot all about the possibilities of what can happen if something went wrong. The deal was set up that evening. Sonny showed up with the money, $100 bills on top and bottom and $1 bills in the middle as planned. At first sight, it looked like a lot of money. Twenty minutes after getting all the rubber bands off of it, the stress factor would set in. They sent me out of the house with the kilo to give Sonny, when he showed up with the money. I would then give the dope to Sonny. Sonny would then give me the money, to give to them. By the time I got into the house, Sonny would be long gone. By the time they opened up the stack of money, this is where one's true acting abilities came in. Soon as I would see the money was fake; it would be time for the Academy Awards Show to begin. I was the one that was left behind, when Sonny left. I would have to show some great acting abilities because, just being a good actor was not enough.

"Oh fuck, that motherfucker, that motherfucker." I would yell out loud. Immediately after this, would come the pacing back and forth and talking to myself saying, "That son of a bitch." All the while I would be balling up my fist and hitting doors and walls in the house. At this time, you could see the victims getting very upset about what had just occurred.

Like I said, just being good at acting wasn't enough. I would then get on the phone and try to call Sonny, who would then say, "fuck you motherfuckers, I got all of you basturds." He would then start laughing on the phone. This dude was a fool. Then I would take these guys to where he might live, at least where I thought he might live. It was all prearranged.

For a good part of the night, I would sit there with them, just as upset as them saying, "I'm going to kill this mother-fucker when I see him." All the while, I was anxious to get home where Sonny was waiting to give me my first kilo. I ended up staying with them about four more hours saying,

"Tomorrow we are going to get together again to look for him." By the next day, they usually accepted the fact that they wouldn't be seeing that kilo again.

When I got home that night, Sonny had given me my first kilo and wasn't asking for any of it. After all, they never got a chance to see who Sonny was or what car he drove. He just wanted to see if I had the balls to do it and he found out that I had—big huge balls. These Mexican guys were just saying to me how this other brother had gotten them for a couple of kilos over two months ago, before this had taken place. They didn't know it at the time, but they were getting set up again.

Man that was pretty easy, or was it? All I had to do was act, so I thought? The next day I would go to school and while I was in class, we were talking about how much you can make as a graduate of Lambson Bussiness College. The top salary back at that time was around $19,000 a year. My thoughts were, as I was thinking about this, *It's going to take me a whole year to make that—shit I'm going to make that over the weekend.* I quit school that day. The next day, I would run into my old soldier named McAllen. We were also former tag team champions from way back. I was very happy to bump into my nigga. He was very happy to see me. I told my nigga, "I need your help to get my operation off the ground," I then said to him, "I found a way to make some real money." Then I took him to my apartment and showed him how much dope I had. His eyes would light up when I told him I got it for free.

McAllen was back on the team immediately. My nigga McAllen was a thoroughbred. He had huge balls and he didn't mind popping a nigga a new asshole. It was just like old times but even better because, we blew up overnight. There was nothing like getting free kilos of dope. The next day, I had to explain to Jesse, my P.O., that I had quit school, so that I could start my own landscaping business.

McAllen was a bad man. Not only did he have the hustling characteristics, he could trim trees better than anyone in the business, in my opinion. This also would be a good way to hide my drug business from Jesse, who would remind me about our first conversation in his office that he was going to let me hang myself. I then told him, "I remember." McAllen was pretty smart, coming up with this one. There would be no question about us coming and going, while they saw work trucks in front of the house.

Jesse called me one day and said, "David, I want to verify your employment." I then said to him, "You can come to this job that I'm doing first thing in the morning." That was the day that I gave a friend of mine a free landscaping job. Since that day, Jesse would never question my work ethics. I paid my monthly P.O. fees and my drug bussiness flourished. I had put together about, $100,000 within several months.

In the year of 1989, this was huge money. We were averaging a free kilo every other week. Drug dealers were coming up short all over the valley. At this point, everybody was jacking, or so it would seem. Sonny and I had an agreement that we wouldn't Jack anyone without giving each other our issues. Sonny would soon violate this agreement several months later and it would be time for the jacker, to get jacked.

At this point, I didn't think times could get any better. I had somewhere around 10 vehicles, which included a Mercedes. This time everything was paid for. We had two houses that I ran in and out of. I had an apartment where I was keeping all the dope. It seemed that everyone was buying dope from me, or was buying dope from someone who was getting it from me. The cash register was ringing every day all day with no restrictions.

I had told McAllen we needed some help, man, since we couldn't get around to everyone. This is when we went to

McAllen's brother's apartment; he was basically living out of a trash can. He was driving a fucked up Ford Pinto, living in a fucked up neighborhood. This nigga was doing badly. I said, "What's up, Dog?" he then said "What's up?" McAllen was saying to his brother, "You remember D, don't you?" He then said, "Yeah."

I felt so bad when I saw how he was living, I said, "Hey man, why don't you come work with us?" McAllen had no idea that I was going to give this nigga a job and he strongly advised me against doing this that night. He flat out told me "D, I know this is my brother, but don't do this D." I said "McAllen, this is your brother man and look how he is living man." He told me again, "D, don't fucking do this." I then reiterated to McAllen, "I put this thing together man, I say who comes and goes me, that's who."

This would prove to be another big mistake that wouldn't blossom until almost 12 months later. This really upset me. McAllen didn't want his own brother to join the team, and I couldn't understand why. Later, I would wish I had heeded his warning. For now, it just looked like McAllen hated his brother.

A few months would go by and things would be going extremely well. I didn't think it really could get much better than this. Then the unexpected came to be. Sonny had set up a deal for that night and the details were kind of weird. It would be the first time I would do a jack and get shot at. Sonny told me, "This guy is supposed to have a kilo and he thinks he is going to jack you, but it's not going to be a whole kilo." I didn't know all the details, but in my mind, this guy was the only one getting jacked. It just so happened that Sonny set the jack move up right around the corner from the house.

I would have McAllen's brother at the house with the side gate open and ready to close it once we drove in the backyard. Sonny would show up that night with three other guys in the car. This was unexpected. I had taken McAllen with me this night, just in case shit got out of hand and it did. Sonny pulled up on this dark street, with the three guys in the car with him. I then approached the car and said to Sonny, "Who's the one selling the drugs?" A guy then answered from the backseat saying, "I got the dope to sell." I then told him, "Show it to me." I was not able to see anybody's face but Sonny's.

At this very moment McAllen was standing right behind me with the 45 auto, just in case things got out of hand. The guy from the backseat of the car who was doing all the talking then handed me what he said was a kilo of the drugs, which looked like a pound instead. After verifying that it was indeed the drug, this guy was making preparations to exit the car. At this very moment, as this guy was starting to stand up out of the car from the backseat, I hit him hard in the jaw. He then fell back into the car. At this point McAllen and I took off running with his drugs in our hands, toward our car. At this very moment, I would hear a loud *boom*! I then yelled to McAllen, "Shoot that son of a bitch!" At this very minute McAllen aimed his gun toward Sonny's car when the guy jumped in the car and Sonny hit the gas and took off. The very next day when Sonny came by, I said to him, "How come you didn't fucking tell me this fucking dude had a gun?" Sonny would then say, "Shit, D. I didn't know he had a gun either. That's why I told him to get in the car and we took off." This would be the first time I actually got shot at, but the unexpected would keep happening.

I had heard Sonny was doing Jacks without kicking me in. Peanut had told me that Sonny had just jacked for three kilos and about 10 pounds. In my mind, this was a major violation, a felony. I said to the guys, "How am I going to be paying this dude on my jacks and then this punk, jacking and not including me in on them." I then said, "Fuck this bitch, and let's go get him." "Greedy," McAllen's brother yelled, "Let's go fuck him up." He appeared to be more upset than me or was just trying to impress me. We loaded up all the guns, including the AK-47 and were already en route, looking for this bitch. We were on the Freeway, when he surprisingly drove right by us. McAllen's brother said, "There's that bitch, follow him."

For the moment he didn't see us, we ended up following him to a restaurant when McAllen's brother jumped out the truck and said, "Hey bitch, where's the dope motherfucker?" I said, "Yeah, we've heard that you've been working without us." He had two other guys with him, who didn't want a part of this. Sonny, was on his own. That's the way it is when you thought you had partner's hanging out with you. When your ass was on the line, you were usually left hanging.

I then looked him in his face and said, "Hey Sonny, where is my issue man and I'm only going to ask you once!" Sonny knew from the look in my eyes, I wasn't playing with him. Sonny said, "D, man, I'm not fucking you over man and I didn't jack for that much." He then said, "I am going to give you 18 ounces and two pounds of weed." We then followed Sonny to his house and picked up our issue or share. This would be our last and final dealing with Sonny. Rumor has it that, Sonny is six feet under. I would never see Sonny again; however, I was in for a few more surprises.

McAllen's brother would turn out to be a good dope seller; we would later label him the Super Server. This nigga would work all night and then bring back all the money, not pinching any for himself. This nigga was better than a hoe would be because, a hoe would get you for something. This nigga was bringing it all back. Needless to say at this point, it was all good. He worked real hard for me and then I rewarded him with a car and then put some rims on it. I then encouraged him to go back out there and keep doing good.

I didn't have to expose myself anymore because, this nigga was taking up all the slack. Pretty soon I trusted him with all my customers. This would later prove to be a fatal mistake. Later this nigga would show why he had no loyalty to anyone, not even his own family member. This nigga would be locked on to the nut sack of anyone he assumed had a lot of money. This is a dirty game. They say, "Don't hate the player, hate the game." It was at this time my name was being heard from east to west, north to south. I remember being in the car with my niggas just driving around when McAllen picked up some freak and I remember McAllen saying to her, "Do you know who Greedy D is?"

"Yeah, I heard of that dude," she said. "They say that nigga was out here making big money." She never realized that I was sitting next to her in the car. That's when I realized that if my name was ringing like that, then the police must be hearing a lot about me, too.

CHAPTER 7

The Destroyer Resurfaces

I had more cars than I could drive, just to clown around in and from time to time, I would park all the cars in front of the house. Looking at everything fixed up, painted up, with rims on, they looked real good. This also looked nice to the police, who were looking to make a buy again from me. They also had our house under surveillance. There was always this one incident in the back of my mind from over a year ago, when I sold dope to this girl whom I had known for at least three years. This guy who she introduced me to looked like the cops. I would then ask him if he was indeed the police. He said no he wasn't.

The police were actually giving smokers dope to smoke, according to the girl who helped to make this possible. She said to me that, they broke her off a piece of the drug for making contact with me. She also told me that she lied when she said he was her cousin and that she was just trying to get a hit that night and that she really didn't know him. They would actually break off a piece of what the smoker would purchase, for hooking them up with that person's drug connection. In this case, I was the drug connection.

Like I said, this is a dirty game. I don't remember the name of the operation, but they had a name for it. In 1987–88, they set up shop on 59th and McDowell at an apartment complex.

In order for the police to make some drug buys, they actually have to become just as dirty as the dope man. The movie *Deep Cover* was a real look at how some of the police lower their standards to get the dope. They have to become just as ruthless as the dope man. Trust me when I say, if the dope man has gotten a lot smarter so have the police. You think that the police can bust some of these major drug loads, by not crossing the line? Think again. Back in these days, they didn't have as many drug-sniffing dogs around, as they do today. A lot of these drug busts required good old fashioned police work. Sometimes the cops actually had gotten their hands dirty. What's seen on TV is the cleaned up version of the war on drugs. What you may see late into the night when the camera isn't rolling could be shocking.

I would later find out on my birthday that he was indeed the police. It was one of those things that you just never forget, when you step on your dick. It looked like food stamps; it was a certified copy. The only problems were I couldn't remember ever filing for some. I will never forget it on that day. We were all drinking at the house, it was my birthday. The music was loud and everybody was feeling really good, drinking as much as they could, until the mailman came. I was fucked up at the time; however, I wouldn't be high anymore once I read the indictment. Needless to say the party would be over immediately, after reading this shit. "Man, damn, fuck." I said. I then said, "I know exactly how this came about. That motherfucking bitch Debra Ann, she did me." Just as bad, two weeks prior, I had spent two nights at the motel with a freak, doing lines all night long. I was off the hook once again.

I knew my P.O. was going to arrest me once he saw me, so I started doing more and more cocaine, with each day that went by that I wasn't incarcerated. I thought, *Fuck he's neverever going to see me again; he's just going to have to catch me.* To make matters even worse, McAllen had gotten back hooked on the drug too. At this point, we had both become addicted to the point of no return.

State of Arizona Versus David Leary, For Sales of Narcotic Drug Cocaine, A Class 2 Felony. "You are hereby ordered to turn yourself in for prints and photographs."

My heart stopped beating for a slight second, as I read this indictment. There was no doubt what this meant. I was going back to prison. Major depression was set back in, which led to more drugs being used and irrational thinking. McAllen and I started going on more cocaine missions with different girls. Every day we were both depressed and fucked up and out of our minds. The sale of cocaine had taken a backseat, and the using of cocaine daily was the present.

Even our drug sales started to fall. One day, we were driving and had stopped at the light wondering, why we weren't making money, like we used to. Just two weeks prior, McAllen's brother had moved out of the house with this girl, when McAllen was just saying, "That's why motherfuckers aren't calling us like they used to, Greedy." His brother then came driving by really fast, looking like he was rushing to one of our customer's houses.

McAllen said, "That's it, D. That motherfucking brother of mine, he's got him a new pager man and he took our clients with him." Then his next words were "D, I told you not to let that motherfucker in, didn't I?" Now he's serving our customers. I felt real stupid as he was talking. He said, "Not only did he take our people, but that nigga is working with the Mexicans across the street from us, they are giving him ounces, and he's rushing them nearly every day for more." I then said, "Those motherfuckers, that bitch." I told McAllen, "I was going to get those Mexicans one day."

I then said to McAllen, "I know those motherfuckers stole our puppies the first day we moved over here, and now in a sense they are selling to our people now, through your fucking brother." I then said, "I owe these Mexicans and I'm going to get them one day, that's a promise." I would later keep my promise.

Major depression was setting in. I couldn't help but to think I was going back to prison again, but this time for a long time. I couldn't get this out of my mind. The only thing that would make me temporarily forget was the constant powdering of my nose with cocaine; however, this would just make me more volatile and crazy. It was time to pay those Mexicans a visit, it was time for some payback. *I'm going to get these fuckers* was my only thought. Most of that morning went to the planning of jacking these fools.

I didn't know what to expect, I didn't care, all I knew was, it was time for them to pay. I probably did somewhere around a quarter-ounce of cocaine that morning, along with a pint of Jack Daniels. I then called this friend of mine who was visiting from California and asked him did he want in? I told him over the telephone, "I am fixing to run into these guys' house, in the next hour during the daytime." He then said, "The daytime?" I said, "Yeah, in the next hour. They won't be expecting it." He then said, "Sure, come by and get me." I went by and picked him up and of course, sucked down some more powder through my nose. *These fuckers are going to get it* was all I could think. We parked our car around the corner and we sneaked around to the house, from the sides.

My friend knocked on the door and surprisingly it was opened. No one looked to see who was on the other side. I then pulled out my 45 auto while saying, "Motherfuckers get on the floor now and don't fucking move."

There were two women and one man and a child in the house. They all got on the floor, while the women were hollering, "Sir, don't shoot, sir don't shoot." I yelled at them, "Where is the fucking dope now?" I then said, "I know it's fucking here."

She then said frightened, "I will show you, sir." I followed her to the back, while my friend kept his gun on the rest. She took me to the cocaine; it was only a quarter of a pound. "Where's the rest?" She then replied, "This is all we have right now." I took it, then we exited the house running to our car, with our guns in our hands, still drawn. "Damn," I shouted to my friend from California, "This is all they had." We then went to his apartment and split up the dope. This showed how bad things had gotten; I was now jacking for small amounts of cocaine. However, they owed and they had drawn first blood by stealing my two Rottie pups and selling drugs to our people. That's a no-no.

This is how the Double Up Boys eventually got ran out of Arizona because, you don't take over another man's turf, without first asking for permission.

McAllen's brother had found out what had gone down by that evening and that's when McAllen gave me a call and said, "Hey man, did you jack them Mexicans?" I then said "Man, they had it coming, dog." He said, "You know my punk ass brother told them that you and I did it." I said, "What? You had nothing to do with it." McAllen states, "My brother sold us out to the Mexicans, for that little bit of dope that they gave him. Now these Mexicans are supposed to be looking for you and I, man." I told my buddy, "Just keep an extra clip." McAllen went on to say, "I hope I never have to kill my own brother." The problem was how do you hurt one brother and then look at the other one for the rest of your life, expecting that he or someone in his family will not take it to the cops?

So at this point I had to leave it alone. McAllen couldn't hurt him either, so the point was moot. Depression would soon set in again, this time at an unprecedented level and paranoia came with it. The police had one of the houses staked out in the rear. It turned out that the police had been watching the house at night for at least two weeks.

We would have never known that, if it wasn't for a lady who lived in the back there, who warned us. One night while on another cocaine binge, I then looked outside the curtain, when I saw a car drive up. In my mind I thought it was those niggas, I immediately grabbed the AK-47. I was sweating tremendously, as I cocked the trigger back while sneaking around the side of the house. It was so dark on this side of the house that they could not see me. *I'm going to kill every one of them* was the thought that was going on inside my mind not realizing, this could be someone else at this particular time. . . .

I had sneaked right up behind them, when I slowly pointed the gun toward the car. With my trigger finger in position to fire this weapon, I pointed the gun, while sweat was pouring down my brawl. It turned out that this was a guy and some lady, who had just stopped there temporarily. All I could think of was *I almost killed them.* I said to myself, "I could have killed someone." No matter how insane I had become, the thought of killing an innocent person didn't sit right with me. They didn't realize that they had been drawn down on with one of the most deadly assault riffles ever made. I was starting to realize how out of reality I had begun to think, after this night.

At this point in my life, praying was the only thing that could help me because, someone was going to die and the possibility of that someone being me was a reality.

At this point, I had people trying to kill me and the thought of knowing that I was probably going to have to kill somebody was taking its toll on me. Everywhere I went, I never kept my back in one position for more then 30 seconds. Needless to say, I was always turning and looking, expecting someone to just come out shooting. I would always go back to using this drug; this is the one thing that would calm my nerves and make me feel good and kind of invincible, at the same time. While on this drug, I was ready for anything, death didn't matter. I was ready for war. While off the drug, reality would set in and I would come to my senses.

The police were probably close to raiding us; however, we moved that weekend. To make matters even worse, we were also at war with some other niggas. They had wanted us to pay them for some money that they had lost in another dope deal that, we had done a couple weeks prior.

At this point, I couldn't go to the bathroom without my pistol and both clips. I had these niggas and the Mexicans looking for me. I found myself hiding out with some freak, doing drugs and having sex. I had gotten to the point that, I wouldn't even come outside unless it was absolutely necessary. I would then go into these crying spells, where I couldn't stop crying, and always afterwards, I would immediately start praying for a cure for this. I wanted to stop using, yet with each time I tried it, I would always end up in failure. At this point, some of my dreams would be about using cocaine and once I would wake up, I would have to have some cocaine and a girl or two, somewhere nearby. I had lost all touch with reality once again. Extreme paranoia had set in; I was doing the drug now, every day all day, without restrictions. I was fucked up in the head, those exact thoughts would continue to repeat themselves in my mind. I was starting to believe that, if something didn't change, someone was going to die.

Between the cocaine missions I would go on, I would remember what my mother told me. *"Son, when it gets too rough son, give it to God, he will fight your battle for you."* Over the course of my life while out in these streets, this would be repeated in my mind. So from point to point in my addiction, I would pray to him, begging him for help, because, I knew at this point, it was going to take someone greater than me to help me through this. The Beast was in total control. However, I had prayed before and I thought nothing had changed. By this time I had overdosed again. *The Lord indeed was hearing my prayers.*

Four days after I was released from the hospital, the Doctor would say to me that "There's nothing more that we can do for you." He then said to me, "If I don't help myself, there's nothing that anyone can do." The problem was that I had tried to help myself before and I would always fail. I had prayed, but I thought God wasn't answering my prayers, yet as I sit here today, I can tell you he was. I just couldn't see it; however, I would never stop asking for help.

CHAPTER 8

Nowhere to Run, Nowhere to Hide

Somehow, I had managed to stay sober for a couple of weeks when I decided that it was time to get out of Arizona. After all I had been here all my life. The other deciding factors were the fact that the police had been looking for me and I still had these people out there trying to kill me. By this time, I had put together a few assets. I figured, it was time to take a break for awhile. After talking to my girlfriend, we both agreed that, it would probably be best for me to leave town. I had been sober for a minute and I was now thinking clearly. I told her, I would have a garage sale and everything from my Mercedes, to the Blazer, to my Monster Pickup Truck, everything must go, even my 69 Chevy Convertible, the one that had been with me since the Car Club days, everything was out of here. Above is just one of the many vehicles that had to go for cheap.

In my mind, I thought I would never return to Phoenix, so I sold everything fast, for at least one half or less than what I had actually paid. I was able to sell everything within three days. Word was out that everything was going cheap. It sold like hotcakes, fast.

I thought it was a time to celebrate on my way out. I even took my boy McAllen and his girl and my girl in a limo to Las Vegas, where we played the slots. However, before the limo started up, I had already crushed up two big rocks with my fingertips and then pushed it up into my nose. The look on everyone's face in the car was that "this nigga is tripping."

Up to this point, I had been clean for while and I had made a promise that I was going to Portland, Oregon, to change my life and to stop doing cocaine. I even paid for different identification cards for McAllen and I. I had a new ID, which said I was James Brown and McAllen would be Earl Jones. We were in the car joking about each other's name and laughing when I was saying to them that I was going to miss Arizona. However, we had not even started up the car to leave Phoenix when I was doing this shit again. No one said anything, but I felt everyone was disappointed in me, for using this shit again. In my mind, I felt I could control it once again, because I had been off it for awhile and it was a time for celebration. I could never have been so wrong.

Let me first to tell you, cocaine and celebration don't mix. Finally, we were on our way to Las Vegas when, I lit up a joint of the half-pound of weed, that I had in my bag. I remember the driver lowering the privacy window, saying "Sir, can you put that out." I then responded "Sure," once he put the window back up, five minutes later, I would light it up again saying, "Fuck him." I then said to McAllen, "I just paid him $700 for this ride. I'm going to smoke, or he can give me my money back, and I will call another limo."

He must have heard me because, the privacy glass didn't lower again until we got to Las Vegas. We played a few slots, then grabbed an airplane to Portland, Oregon, where my girlfriend's grandad was waiting with open arms. Once we had gotten to Oregon, my girl's grandfather showed us around town, when he stopped at the store in his neighborhood to grab change. A familiar scene would soon be staring me in the face. That's when I noticed there must have been 10 guys on the corner selling dope and dressed in all red. They were flamed up, even the shoes.

I had a lot of money on me at the time, so needless to say, I was a little concerned. They were making their money in plain view, which reminded me of the Double Up Boys. They sell double.

It didn't take more than about three days, for the girls to become homesick and return to Phoenix, which left me and McAllen there alone. It didn't take long for me to start losing my fucking mind again. I had been cracked by a tramp, for the nearly new Iroc Z28, which I had just bought. This bitch was in the car and I was at the motel high and out of my fucking mind. I didn't even know this tramp and I have given up the car. Hours would go by when McAllen would come to the motel and say "Greedy, you are fucking tripping man. You mean to tell me, you gave the car to a bitch you don't know?"

McAllen went and tracked the car down and brought it back to the studio apartment that we shared. It wouldn't be long when the money would be close to running out. So I then jumped on an airplane and flew back to Phoenix and picked up some more dope and then went back to Portland to sell it. This never really worked long-term because, each time we would get more dope, I would go on another binge with some freak. I would go to motel rooms and damn near fuck it all off, until we were buying small amounts. I messed off the money in Oregon, so I didn't have the money to return to Phoenix to get more drugs.

Things were getting really bad again and the worst was still yet to come. Once again after being out with one of those tramps again for several days, I then came back broke, with no money and no dope. I would go into a serious depression and then start crying uncontrollably and saying "Why can't I quit this and why hasn't God answered my many prayers?" I didn't know it, nor was it in the realm of possibility that God was indeed looking out for me. *I shouldn't ever question him!*

I was alone in this apartment, just crying uncontrollably, my heart beating very rapidly, while saying over and over again, "Why can't I quit this, Lord God?" I continued to pray over and over again. My soul was hurting something fierce. "Why can't I quit this dear, Lord God," was my plea. Forty-five minutes would pass by and I was still in tears and hurting so badly and stinking, thinking this isn't the son my mother wanted me to be. It was at this time, I thought that God wasn't hearing me, while saying these very words inside of my mind, *Why can't I quit this dear Lord?* My life was locked into a battle between good and evil. At one point I couldn't stop crying. I was in mental pain and anguish from doing these drugs, over the years. I couldn't help to think of how badly my life had turned out; I was a nothing; a nobody, a failure. *Glory to God, most merciful and forever loving!*

Then something happened that I would never forget for the rest of my life. I got up off the floor while wiping the tears off my face. I had probably been on the floor some 30 to 45 minutes. I was stinking and needed a shower, when I took off all my clothes and then jumped into the shower. Immediately after stepping out of the shower door, I looked at a towel on the door that I didn't remember putting there.

There at that very minute was now a presence in that room that was so strong my body began to hive and bump up. I was afraid. I remember grabbing the same pants that I had just taken off, while looking around in the bathroom to see who was there, but I couldn't see anyone. I could feel someone other than me was there, no doubt about it. I would not take my back off the wall. I remember moving forward, with my back scraping against the wall. This presence was so strong, so real and so powerful that, I could actually feel it, but I couldn't see anything. This scared the living heck out of me.

I lived in a studio apartment, where you could see everything, except for the bath area. I could feel something in here, but I could see no one. This presence was in the room and it felt so strong to me, so real to me. I was very much afraid because, I saw no one. I remember looking around the wall from the bathroom area, while my back was pinned against the wall. The presence grew stronger with each second that would go by and I became more afraid. I became more fearful of what I could not see. The presence grew stronger and stronger. With each minute that I was in the room, the presence grew stronger, to the point where, I then grabbed my shirt and then ran out the room, very much in fear of the unknown. The unseen.

I wouldn't go back into the apartment until some two hours later. There was just no way I was going back in there, until McAllen had come. I remember sitting out on the stairs, when McAllen came home. He said, "Greedy, what's up dog?" He then said before I could answer, "Why are you out here?" I then told him of the presence that was inside and that I was afraid to go back in. He kind of looked at me not believing me and smiling like, right. He then walked inside and said "D, there is nobody inside of here? D, you are tripping." I then stuck my head in the door and the presence was gone.

That's when I said to McAllen, "I'm ready to go back home man and turn myself in to the police." I remember telling McAllen that I was tired of living my life in this manner. That it was time for a change. McAllen had agreed and we made preparation to return to Phoenix, within the next two days. I had no idea of how change was coming; I just knew change was needed.

Portland, Oregon, was so beautiful, so pretty and green, just the opposite of Phoenix, so dry and brown. These two States would share something in common. They both had a drug problem in which in the aftermath, there would be death and total devastation. For the ones that survived, they would always linger on the thought of going back to using. Cocaine, meth, Ecstasy and heroin are very dangerous drugs.

Drugs, they mess with you in your sleep. Even if you kick the habit, you have to now deal with the after effects of the drug. When you are not thinking of the drug consciously, you are thinking of it subconsciously. Once I would dream about using it, by the time I would wake up, I would have to have it. This is the one thing that most addicts can't fight, especially when the thought of sex is then introduced, while you are dreaming about it. You are basically insane at this point and nothing would stop the average user from getting high again. It's especially hard, when you are craving the sex and the drug at the same time, especially if he or she is new to recovery. There is no treatment for this. This would put these drugs, in a category of the most dangerous drugs ever invented. This is why in my opinion, the treatment facilities stay full. There is always a waiting list to get in these places unless you are the president of the United States or someone of importance.

That morning McAllen and I headed out, back to Phoenix. McAllen, still had a half-ounce of cocaine with him. I then said to him, "Give it to me." I put it in my socks, inside the suitcase that was placed inside the trunk of the car. We were on the Freeway, when we stopped in Los Angeles, at McAllen sister's house. McAllen then got out of the car, suggesting that he would meet me in Phoenix later. Even McAllen couldn't put up with my bullshit any more. I would then start the trip alone, back to Phoenix from Los Angeles. I remember stopping at my first rest stop, which was just a few mile from Los Angeles when I remembered, I still had the half-ounce in my suitcase, inside one of my socks. The dope was so good to me that, after being off of it for a couple of days, at every rest stop, I would get out of my car and go into the suitcase and grab a few more little packages of it. At one point I had reached into the bag and taken a big powder rock and squeezed it, while thrusting it up my nose, when a couple had pulled up beside me. They looked over at me and saw my eyes bulging out of my head and cocaine residue all around my nose.

This probably scared the shit out of them. They became frightened and hit the gas, trying to get away from me However, in my mind, it looked as if they were trying to race me. I know now that they were trying to get away from me. Just the look on my face, with cocaine all around my nose and eyes bulging out; I probably scared them half to death. I kept following them down the Freeway and they kept trying to get away from me. They would later lose me. I was all alone when the sign on the Freeway read, Blythe California Exit ahead, 2 miles. I remember reaching into the little bag and grabbing the rest of the cocaine and then crushing it with my fingertips, then pushing it up my nose when, I looked in the rearview mirror saying, "Shit, it's a motorcycle cop!" At a distance, I could see him with his lights on and in my opinion, he was coming fast my way. I remembered that, I had more cocaine still in my suitcase, in the trunk.

I figured I would outrun him. I then mashed the gas and took off towards the Blythe California Exit. I had to be going somewhere around 80 miles per hour at this time, when I noticed up the street, after I had gotten off the exit, the police had the street blocked off. So I remember driving through this big huge orange orchard, when I heard some people yelling, "Hey get out of here." I kept going as fast as I could when I ran out of road. I then stopped the car and got out on foot. It had to be around nine that night and I could see the police car lights surrounding the orchard at every corner and they were getting out on foot and with dogs that I could hear barking.

It was pitch dark out there and I was higher then a motherfucker. I then snatched off the white shirt that I was wearing. Here I was, in the middle of this field high, my heart pounding in my chest, not just from doing the cocaine, also from the excitement and the running.

They had so many cops out in this field looking for me that, it appeared to be the whole police department. I remember hiding by this bush and praying to God, not to let them send me back to prison. I wanted to see my newborn daughter, Raven, whom I wanted so desperately to see one more time. By this time, my eyes were still bulging out of my head. Actually my eyes were even bigger now because the police were involved.

I was trying to catch my breath after running, which was very difficult because of all of the excitement and my usage. I was finding it a little hard to breathe. A cop had just walked right by me, but he didn't see me. I kept my head down, when I lifted my head up again all I could see was a bunch of flashlights, going in all kind of directions. All of a sudden a light hits me square in the eyes, "Motherfucker put your hands up now, or I will blow your fucking brains out!" the cop yelled.

I had to think fast. I had remembered an old friend of mine who told me, "If you ever have to run from the cops and they catch you and you have cocaine on you, then use this story, it will work." I remembered those words at this time, I began yelling,"Please don't hit me!" I immediately went into one of my Grammy Award Winning Roles. "Please officer, don't hit me." "The only reason I ran was, I thought you guys were going to beat me up," I said to him. I explained that I had been beaten by you all before, citing issues with racism." I just kept repeating, "Please, officer, don't hit me. Please don't hit me, please!" By this time they had my fake ID saying I was James Brown, so they continued to question me by that name. At one point, I was put into the backseat of the police car when, I could see them going through my suitcase. "Oh man," I said quietly, "they are going to find the drugs." However, I had put on a good show, with the side show, don't hit me routine, that they didn't do an extensive search that would have yielded the drugs.

So the plan did work; however, now I was on my way to the Blythe California County Jail. I knew once I had gotten there, they would do fingerprints and find out who I really was. Still I didn't really know at this time, if they had found the drugs. The police were keeping quiet about everything. Immediately while entering the county jail, I felt really sick. I didn't know what was happening, all I knew was my heart was still pounding in my chest, my eyes still bulging out and I was feeling light-headed. I remember one of the cops saying to me "Mr. Brown, you don't look good at all" and the last thing I remember saying to him was, "I don't feel good either." Right when I said that, I was unconscious according to the cop who I remembered hearing, as I had regained my senses. "Mr. Brown, are you okay? Mr. Brown, are you okay?" the cop would continue to ask.

At this point, I was on my way to a hospital. They had explained to me that I have had a seizure. This is when I noticed that just about every tooth was loosened in my mouth. I felt week and very tired. I remember finally getting to the hospital when, one cop came in and got my thumb print, while I was lying there in the hospital bed. I knew soon, if I didn't get going, they would find out who I really was and then arrest me.

Two more hours had gone by when, the Cop looked at me and said "Mr. Brown, are you ready to go back to jail?" I said to him, "I guess if I have to." I got ready to climb out of the bed when again, that's all I remembered. I blacked out again, I had had another seizure. But this time was different; my stomach had knotted up in little bumps and then one big knot that is still visible to this day. *This knot would be there, in my stomach forever more, to remind me of the Lord God, bringing me out of bondage.*

By this time the police department didn't want to have anything else to do with me. They left me in the care of the hospital. I remember asking the cop, "Where is my car?" He said, "At some gas station." I remember telling this cop "I'm not from here." He then said to me, "You're going to have to look it up." He was being a prick. While lying there in the Hospital bed for another half hour, I then said to the doctor, I'm fixing to go. He then said to me that he wouldn't advise it because, I could have another blackout and kill some one on the Freeway." I then said to him, "I got to go," remembering they had my fingerprints and they could easily find out who I am and even worse, what if they had found the cocaine.

I took my time getting out of the hospital bed this time; I surely didn't want to fall out again. Once I had gotten out of the hospital door, I saw another cop when I explained to him my situation and begged him to just take me to where my car was. The cop ended up dropping me off in front of the garage that had my car. I remember talking to two males who were working there when I asked, "Where's my car?" They said to me, "it must have come in last night," I said "yeah." Then they asked, "What happened?" I told them, " I was riding on the Blythe California Highway, while doing some cocaine when a motorcycle cop started chasing me with his lights on."

One of the guys then said, "That must be some good dope dude!" I said "Yeah it is." He then said, "Dude, there are no motorcycle cops in Blythe, California." I then said, "What you are kidding me, right?" He said, "No dude, you were hallucinating." I then said "Damn!" The other guy confirmed what the dude said, "There's no motorcycle cops in Blythe." I then ran to my suitcase, to find the drugs were still there. The police didn't find them!

I then asked one of the guys, "Could he fill my car up with gas?" He said, "As long as we can trade for some of that cocaine you got?" I said, "Sure." We made the trade, then I was on my way back to Phoenix. Along the way, I would keep looking down at the knots, wondering why they weren't going away in my stomach.

I wouldn't do anymore of the drugs all the way home, because of this. I didn't know what was going on, with my stomach. I still felt kind of strange, like I could have another seizure at any time, so I took my time coming into Phoenix. Once I had gotten to Phoenix, I was supposed to have been making preparations for turning myself into prison. However; the destroyer would have his way first.

I went back to Phoenix and back to my girlfriend and daughter. I had been nearly sober for three weeks; however, the knots in my stomach were still there. I was concerned because they didn't look like they would be going away, any time soon. All of the sudden, I started getting the urges to use again.

With each hour that went by, the urges grew stronger and even worse, the thoughts of using were in my dreams. Also the need for sex grew stronger, but not with my girlfriend. I wanted sex with a stranger, which made the thoughts of using cocaine again, even more difficult to deal with. It was like the phone kept ringing and I was trying not to answer. It just kept calling me and there was nothing I could do about it. In my mind I wanted it to stop ringing, but it wouldn't. The phone calls wouldn't stop in my mind until I had to answer. Even worse, when I went to sleep, now it was in my dream. The thought of dealing with this on a conscious level was hard to deal with, now I was dreaming about it, which was even harder. After waking up from my dream of using the drug and having sex with some female, it would almost insure my quest, the very next day of using more cocaine or meth, or whatever I could come up with first.

The next day, I would be looking for one of my old freaks, after trading my AK-47 for an ounce of the drug, or even worse, I would be looking up and down Van Buren Street, which is known for pimps and prostitution. While on the drug, nothing excited me more than a different sexual partner. Once again, I was losing my fucking mind. I was running up and down Van Buren in my car, looking for a hoe, because I couldn't locate any of my old freaks. I knew better about fucking with the hoes and tramps walking down the streets; however, I wasn't in the driver's seat. I was being led by the thought of doing cocaine, while having sex with a different woman. *This is just one of the many dangers of doing this drug.*

What's crazy about this was, I had a girlfriend and a child at home. I didn't need to be in the streets, looking for a freak. Once the cocaine had been ingested, nothing was rational about the decisions I was making. This type of behavior was dangerous for me and my woman. I knew this because, there were so many different diseases in the streets. But nothing would matter, when I took that first hit. I was dangerous to anybody that came into my zone. In many cases, I was a walking cluster fuck who could care less about anybody's feelings, including my very own. The drug was once again making my decisions. *The beast was once again in total control.*

It didn't take long for me to run out of money and out of the good graces of my girlfriend. Most of the time, she couldn't account for where I was, which led to a certain amount of suspicions. This also would lead to a lot of fights. This woman truly loved me and did everything she could to help me and more.

She just didn't know that, no matter what she did, it would never be enough. Our relationship was destined to fail because the drug was calling all the shots, so to say. This drug took a toll on her as well. I remember the talks she would have, about taking her car and driving it as fast as she could into a brick wall. I used to make her cry a lot, she gave it her all and it would not be good enough. Her mom's addiction was also taking a toll on her which is another story within itself. She had been dealing with my addiction and with her mother's, which would soon make her mentally unstable. Dealing with an addicted boyfriend was bad, dealing with your addicted mother was even worse. She was living in hell and at the time, I could care less about how she felt. No matter how much I would promise her that I would change, I couldn't live up to my many promises. In a sense, it would seem that I was a natural born loser.

CHAPTER 9

Prison, My Destiny

November 13, 1990

"David stand against the wall, spread your legs, now stand over here so we can get your picture," the guard yelled. Once again I was in the Horse Shoe at the Maricopa County Jail. The Horse Shoe is a motherfucker! Here you get a chance to look at society's rejects. I got a chance to look at people just like myself, who had lost all hope. There were many just like me who had burnt all bridges. All had fallen from grace. I knew I was looking at a lot of time after all, I was already on probation when I sold drugs to an undercover cop.

Nearly three months had gone by when I called home to talk to my girlfriend; I will never forget those words, "Hey you are not going to believe this." I said, "What?" "She then said, I had a talk with Rolo's uncle last night and he said Rolo was an undercover informant back in 1986 and 1987." Immediately after hanging up the phone with her, the mystery puzzle of when I got raided back in 1987 by the police came together.

Rolo was the one who did me, he was the only thought that came into mind. All I could think of was, *I want his blood for this! That bitch, he couldn't hold is own, so he brought it to me, that son of a bitch.* Once again my heart became hardened. He knew my mom and I let him come over with different girls to the house I had. This is the thanks I got. *How could he do this to me?* is the thought that I couldn't get out of my mind. I wanted his blood for this; I wanted it so badly I could taste it.

Coincidentally, I would see Rolo the next day while in the recreation pin, inside the county jail. A glass, steel door stood in between us. I walked up to the door, showing no emotions on my face whatsoever, when I said to him, "Hey

RICHARD M. ROMLEY
MARICOPA COUNTY ATTORNEY

ROBERT E. KNAPP
BAR ID #: 010957
Deputy County Attorney
111 West Monroe, Suite 1800
Phoenix, AZ 85003
Telephone: 602 262-1124
Attorney for Plaintiff

QUADRANT UA

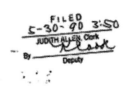

FILED
5-30-90 3:50
JUDITH ALLEN, Clerk
By _____ Deputy

DR. 89-082067 PPD

IN THE SUPERIOR COURT OF THE STATE OF ARIZONA

IN AND FOR THE COUNTY OF MARICOPA

STATE OF ARIZONA,	)	CR90- 06012
Plaintiff,	)	121 GJ 153
vs.	)	INDICTMENT
DAVID LEARY,	)	SALE OF NARCOTIC DRUGS, A CLASS 2 FELONY
Defendant.	)	

The Grand Jurors of Maricopa County, Arizona, accuse DAVID LEARY, on this 30th day of May, 1990, charging that in Maricopa County, Arizona:

DAVID LEARY, on or about the 8th day of June, 1989, knowingly transported for sale, imported into this state or offered to transport for sale or import into this state, sold, transferred or offered to sell or transfer cocaine, a narcotic drug, in violation of A.R.S. §§ 13-3408, 13-3401, 13-701, 13-702, 13-801, and 13-812.

_____
("A True Bill")

RICHARD M. ROMLEY
MARICOPA COUNTY ATTORNEY

_____
ROBERT E. KNAPP
DEPUTY COUNTY ATTORNEY

RK/dm/AO
522.9/jd

Date: May 30, 1990

_____
LAWRENCE W. GRAESSLEY
FOREMAN OF THE GRAND JURY

THE STATE OF ARIZONA ·	CAUSE NO. CR9006012 & PV CR8702391
Plaintiff	
	HONORABLE THOMAS M. O'TOOLE
vs.	
	CRIMINAL DIVISION H
DAVID ALLEN LEARY	
Defendant	SUPERIOR COURT

PRESENTENCE AND PROBATION VIOLATION REPORT

PRESENT CHARGE: **Cause No. CR9006012:** Sale of Narcotic Drugs, a Class 2 Felony, as originally charged.

PROB. VIOL. CHARGE: **Cause No. PV CR8702391:** Count I: Possession of Narcotic Drugs for Sale, Cocaine, a Class 2 Felony. Originally charged as Count I: Possession of Narcotic Drugs for Sale over $250.00, a Class 2 Felony, and Count II: Possession of Marijuana for Sale, a Class 4 Felony.

PLEA: **Cause No. CR9006012:** April 8, 1991.
Cause No. PV CR8702391: November 23, 1987.

CUSTODY STATUS:

Cause No. CR9006012:

Dates of Incarceration	Reasons For Incarceration	Days In Custody
11-14-90 to 5-7-91	Presentence	175
	Total	175

Cause No. PV C88702391:

Dates of Incarceration	Reasons For Incarceration	Days In Custody
3-10-87 to 3-11-87	Presentence	2
4-15-87 to 4-17-87	Presentence	3
1-4-88 to 2-17-88	Term #15	45
11-14-90 to 5-7-91	Probation violation	175
	Total	225

DEFENSE COUNSEL: Joel Hoffman, privately retained.

PRESENT OFFENSE:

The following information is taken from Phoenix Police Departmental Report #89-082067:

PAGE 1

```
NAME      DAVID ALLEN.LEARY                RACE B      SEX M      HT 5'11"
RESIDENCE 225 H. Madison                   EYES Bro    HAIR Blk   WT 225
          Phoenix, Arizona    ZIP 85007    DOB 6-11-61            AGE 29
PHONE                MESSAGE PHONE None     CITIZEN OF USA
AKA OR MAIDEN None                          BIRTHPLACE Phoenix, AZ
ID MARKS        Scars on chest              DRIVER'S LIC. NO. Suspended
EMPLOYER/ADDRESS/PHONE Unemployed           S.S. NO.                      FILED
                                            FBI NO. 837088HA3         MAY 15 1991
OCCUPATION Landscaper   EDUCATION 20        BOOKING NO. 264015        JUDITH ALLEN, Clerk
MARITAL    Putative     RELIGION Christian  CHILDREN 1
                                                                      By
                                                                          Deputy
```

CURRENT OFFENSE

```
CAUSE NO. CR9006012      OFFENSE DATE 6-8-89                 NCIC 3540N
  CHARGE Sale of Narcotic Drug, a Class 2 Felony
A.R.S. NOS. 13-3408, 3401, 701, 702, 801, 812
CAUSE NO. PV CR8702391   OFFENSE DATE 3-10-87                NCIC 3555N
  CHARGE Ct I: Possession of Narcotic Drugs for Sale, Cocaine, a Class 2
         Felony
A.R.S. NOS. 13-3406, 3401, 701, 702, 801, 812

DATE OF ARREST 11-14-90                    ARRESTING AGENCY PHPD
DATE INCAR. 11-14-90       REL. DATE                REL. STATUS J
DAYS IN JAIL THIS ARREST 175  REMAND JUVENILE COURT/DATE--NO

DEFENSE COUNSEL Joel Hoffman, private      PROSECUTOR Robert Knapp
GUILT BY/DATE     Plea/4-8-91         SENTENCING JUDGE THOMAS O'TOOLE
DATE OF SENTENCE 5-8-91
COOEF/DISPOS None
```

CRIMINAL HISTORY			WARRANTS OUTSTANDING		
			CASE NO.	CHARGE	STATE
NO. CONVICTIONS:	FEL 1	MISD	JUV		
NO. INCARCERATIONS:	PRISON 1	JAIL 1			
	ESCAPE	OTHER			
NO. SUPERVISIONS:	PROB 1	PAROLE	OTHER:		

GENERAL INFORMATION

```
NARCOTICS/ALCOHOL HISTORY PA-Alcohol/PU-Marijuana/PU-Methamphetamin./A-Cocaine
TREATMENT/PROGRAMS New AZ Family/Terros/AA/NA

MILITARY HISTORY NOT APPLICABLE
  BRANCH                        TYPE DISCH.
  ENTRY DATE                    DISCH. DATE
```

SPOUSE/RELATIVES/CHILDREN

NAME	RELATION	AGE	ADDRESS	PHONE
Katherine Johnson	mother	63	1650 E. Cambridge, #5116, Phx., AZ	None

0492S/04-30-91/jcl

Rolo, you bitch, I'm going to kill you when I get out of here!" After I said this to him, he immediately blamed Big Harry for what happened back in 1987. The only problem was he wasn't supposed to already know why I was going to kill him. I never explained why to him and I hadn't seen him in three years before this. I just told him, I was going to kill him. I promised him that, he wouldn't live to grow old. At this point in my life, I didn't respect anyone who couldn't live with the shit that they had created. Rolo was on intensive probation at the time, when he had gone back to jail. I had to kill him for this one.

Anyone knows that back in those days, when you were on intensive probation and you violated probation, there was no just getting out of it. You had a mandatory prison sentence coming. Rolo had gotten out of jail, while on intense. This was a red flag; however, I was doing so much of the dope that I couldn't pay attention to everyone in my surroundings. This is how sneaky bastards like this would sneak in for the kill. He played me like a piano.

Now I forgive him because, cocaine destroyed him, like it destroyed me. How could someone continue to beg God for forgiveness and it be granted, but you are not able to forgive? How do you beg for mercy and you are not willing to give it? However, back then, the dope was still in my system, there was no doubt in my mind, I would have killed this man for this and he knows this.

Six months nearly had gone by. My girlfriend wasn't answering the phone like she used to and all old friends had changed their numbers. Even worse, I was getting ready to be sentenced by the courts. I kept calling the number at the house when finally, I reached my girlfriend and verified what I already suspected, she already found another boyfriend, which hurt. What can I say? I had it coming.

April 1, 1991—It Was Time to Make My Transition From Jail, to the Big House

It was time to pay some dues that had been way overdue. Now, it was time to see who your friends really were. Now it was time to be a man, David.

"David Leary," the judge said, "are you here to plead guilty to the charges of conspiracy to sell cocaine, a Class 2 Felony and Possession of a Narcotic Drug for sale, also a Class 2 Felony?" "Yes Sir!" "David Leary, I hereby sentence you to the Department of Corrections, for a flat sentence of six years, with time served for jail time." The judge then hit the gavel down. I looked to the left, my lawyer was already gone. He never said one word to me, I just looked over and he was out of there. *That piece of shit, that son of a bitch,* is all I could think at that time. *I actually paid him for this. I could have gotten better service from a public pretender,* were my thoughts. The term for public defender, back in those days. As a matter of fact, not one person I knew was there other than my friend Chow's brother, whom he sent because he couldn't be there. I then looked back to see how many family members came, not one soul. I was so hurt by this, but could I really blame them? I had burnt every bridge.

All hope had been lost, now it was time to see what I was really made of. I went back to my cell that evening, somewhat in a transformation. All I could think of was, *I can't believe that, I'm going away for six long years!* I remember telling my thoughts to this other guy named Steven, who had been sentenced that day as well. He asked me "D, how much time you got man?" I told him, "Six fucked up years," with anger visibly on my face. He then said very sadly, "They gave me 40 years man." He said, "As a matter of fact, I don't want to hear about your six years, no more man!" I had problems, but this guy really had problems, he was only 20 at the time. I had lost everything that I thought was important. I had also burnt all bridges. All my friends had eventually changed their numbers. On top of all of this, another man was helping to raise my daughter.

I had been broken down in spirit. Now, it was time for the Lord to start working on me, but I would not give in easily because, I didn't know he was reaching out to me at the time. *His way is the truth and the life.*

One week after I was sentenced, I was at Central Intake, at the Department of Corrections. I had made it to the Big House. Eventually, I would have to show my fighting skills, whether real or imaginary. I was locked up with a bunch of dudes in one room, while going through intake. This many people in one room, I knew it was time to start getting my swoll on because, it's always going to be some shit, at one point or another. A strong defense is just as good as a strong offense. So I immediately started lifting water bags, while anticipating getting to the prison yard, to hit the pig iron.

I wasn't a gang member, so I knew this alone would bring about problems for me and I was determined by the time I got to the prison yard, to go straight to the weight pile.

I watched the big prison bus pull up two weeks after being at Central Unit. It was a long ride to the prison shackled up like some animal from the waist down to the bus. We weren't going anywhere until we got to our destination, that's for sure. Once we got to Florence, which is basically one big prison with a lot of little prisons that work together with only one purpose, to keep you locked down. It was time to start actually doing time. I would soon see true suffering, but in a different perspective. If you don't get any love from the streets, it's extremely hard in prison. I would soon find that out. I would soon meet more guys like me, who had lost all hope just like me, who now had a number, which would be their identification for years to come, just like me.

Supermax Prison, The Big House, C-B-8

My first stop was the CB-8 Super Max Unit. They took pride in this prison. Nobody could escape here; even an attempt could get you killed. They had orders to shoot and no officer that I met had a problem with this. They keep people like the Breenawalts here and Robert Sackers. Like Sackers, who came here originally with a five-year sentence, he ended up killing one or two of his cell mates over the years. Now he's serving a life sentence.

I believe he is on Death Row. In here, if you are not smart, you will allow someone to think for you, as I would soon find out. One could end up making it a lifetime commitment, when they enter the prison system. Just like Sackers. If you want and are looking for death, you could get it here; there is no need to look any further. Over on Death Row, it was so quiet in that area every day. We couldn't walk down that area however, it reminded me of being in a mortuary. There was no doubt, death lingered within these walls. However, at the front of the prison, we saw juveniles running in what appeared to be 120-degree weather with a log on their backs and sweating like dogs.

It was hotter than a motherfucker on the bus. These guys were actually running as fast as they could, with no shirt on their back in the heat. No trees to cover you, just desert. They were in this new program called "SHOCK." This is actually what they did. They shocked the shit out of you and your ass, back into reality.

They housed these guys at CB-8 which had just been built. At this time this was the mother of all prisons in Arizona. This is where if you wanted drama, they had drama for your ass. Before we actually got in the front doors, I knew I wasn't going to like it there. For someone like me, who was hard-headed and unwilling to listen, this was the right place for me to start out. In a sense, I needed a "SHOCK," too.

Orientation came that same day; they piled us all in this room still handcuffed. This is how orientation started off. Man, this is a good place to get your ass kicked if need be, the officer implied. Then it was the showing of a video clip of an inmate who needed his ass kicked and their delivering on that promise. They beat the shit out of this guy.

Somehow, I knew this wouldn't be for me, so I would immediately have respect for the system and the situation I was in. After about another hour of being intimidated for the first time in my life, I was then stripped of my clothes. They wanted to look up our asses, this was humiliating to me and we were then shipped off to the cells where we would be staying. They made us work in the kitchen and they would let us hit the pig iron. Needless to say, I hit it every day—I wasn't going to be someone's bitch. Nor, was I going to get bullied by some gang. I knew problems were headed my way because of the lifestyle, at this point in which I was leading. When these young fuckers came in there they were already afraid, most joined a gang.

I chose to walk it alone. I always figured that I would eat four meals a day and lift weights every single time given the opportunity. From doing this I had quickly swelled up. My chest, arms and legs grew. I lifted that iron daily. By the time I got out of prison, I wanted to be the biggest and the strongest.

In prison, the punishment is not just in confinement. It would come in your mattress, which is only about four inches thick and then you sleep on iron every day. If you have a bad back, you are just shit out of luck without a doctor's excuse as the warden would put it to me. "David, what makes you better than anybody else?" he asked with this shit-eating grin on his face. "You get nothing."

At this time, I was pleading for an extra mattress. You also had to adapt to the rats, which would sneak in while we were sleeping at night to eat your food. Sometimes the rats were so desperate and hungry that they would climb up by your head, searching for food. There was also a light that never went off at night that was just above your head. You could hear the power actually going through it, at night while you were sleeping. This too would prove to be annoying. Over here they would bring the hardest of the hardest to do time. The term locking you up and throwing the key away existed here at this prison. I remember talking to a guy who had been in lock-down for two years and he started crying while eating his food at the table saying, "These motherfuckers are going to lock me down for another year!" Like if it was something that we could do for him?

Lockdown means just that, no movement. I would watch men turn into animals including myself. Some people were in lockdown 24 hours a day, every day for years. Also, the punishment came in the meal. If you are used to eating good, prison is no place for you. When I think of the prison food I think of Wackenhutt. It really turns my stomach. They got this pizza which I called it, day old cornbread, with ketchup on it. This is what they would serve you at some prisons every

Sunday. If I didn't have food that I stole from the kitchen or bought from the store, I was dieting that day.

One month had gone by and it was time for the shit to get started. This guy Junior Flip had already warned this Mexican guy to turn his TV down in the mornings when he was going to work. Junior Flip forgot for a minute that we weren't living at Motel 6. Junior Flip told the Mexican guy that when he got back from work, he was fixing to get in his ass. The way Junior sounded, it seemed like the Mexican should have started packing his stuff up and asked the guards to take him to the hole, which would be a no-no for an inmate. Junior Flip really was convincing.

Junior told him, "When you get back, get ready to get your ass kicked." The only problem was Junior didn't work out as hard as this Mexican did. Junior Flip would be in his room watching soap operas, while the recreation session was in motion. I used to see the Mexican out running in the heat, while punching in the air, then back on the weight pile. I will never forget it.

We were in the recreation area in our pod, playing a game of Dominos. Junior Flip was sitting there with his gloves on the table for everyone to see, while waiting on the Mexican to come back, so he can get into his ass, as promised. Junior really looked like he was going to whip some tail. Sometimes one's appearance can be misleading. Anyways, the Mexican guy came back that evening as expected. When Junior Flip saw him coming through the gate, he started putting on his gloves while signaling at the Mexican and saying, "Come on bring your ass!"

Both guys went into the pen along with Junior's roommate and I, to make sure that no one else jumped in. Two men enter, one man limps out or is carried out is the name of the game. Only one would emerge as winner and I can assure you, it wouldn't be Mr. Flip.

Before Junior could block any of the punches, three or four had landed plush on his dome. Junior couldn't block everything that was being thrown at him. Junior's roommate and I looked at each other while saying to ourselves, "Damn." Now junior was lumped up when he then went into wrestling mode. He wasn't successful with this either. Now Junior was on the ground knotted up and bleeding looking at me saying, "Big Dog, get him." This is what can happen, when one forgets where he is.

I then said to Junior Flip, "Nigga, you just got your ass whipped!" Then the Mexican guy was standing over Junior saying, "Motherfucker, you want some more?" With his fist still balled up. Junior then said again, "Big Dog, get him." I then looked over at the Mexican guy and told him, I have no problems with you, this was a fair fight. The Mexican was worried because he had just beaten down a friend of ours. For nearly two weeks afterwards, Junior Flip wouldn't emerge from his room.

As a matter of fact, after that ass whipping, Mr. Flip was a very peaceful man, a humble man. I didn't realize that my time at Super Max would be brief. I don't believe I stayed there more than three months. One evening over the loudspeaker, I would hear "Leary, roll up Leary 65798," as the voice echoed in the building. I didn't know where I was going. One thing for sure, trouble was headed my way again and because, I was hard-headed, there was nothing I could do to avoid it. When you allow people to think for you, you are prone to get into trouble. Eventually, I would be forced to start thinking for myself.

Ryening Unit, Cell Block 9
Florence, Arizona

I had been a good boy over at C-B-8. Now, I had been granted more freedom, I'm finally in a lower custody yard. Now, I got to come out of my cell a good part of the day. Because, I had been hardened by the lifestyle of living in the projects, I figured that there wouldn't be too much that could really bother me. I had seen and done a lot of bad shit. I figured that I had seen it all. I was wrong. I wasn't totally prepared for what was going to happen next. I thought I was quick on my feet, but this guy was quicker, even worse he was a cop. I will never forget this fucker.

I had been warned over a great part of my life, to never trust someone who's always smiling, someone that wears a shit-eating grin every time you see him, because trust me, life is just a little more complicated than that. Sometimes in life, the unexpected could come and take the smile off of anyone's face; this took the smile off of mine. The bus stopped in front of the building.

"Alright, everyone off this bus!" The guard yelled with his gun pointed at us. They then escorted us off the bus and then hoarded us like cattle into this building. Once they took the handcuffs off, it was time for them to look up in our asses, once again. It was time to take away our manhood, once again. Like I've said, I've seen and done a lot of bad things, but this was one thing that would prove hard to get used to. After this insult, we were then given our clothes and were told to walk to our pods. This white cop who had handed me my clothes was smiling when he gave them to me. He then said, "How are you doing?" I responded by saying, "Cool." I thought he was being cool, because he admired my big guns, my arms. If you were large in size, some cops respected you, or so I thought? The very next day, we were given orientation.

I would see this same cop again, smiling and being real cool. I would see him again, serving me a plate a food in the chow hall later, just smiling all the time, trying to be real cool with me. By this time we had started talking back and forth. He was asking me, where did I come from and stuff like that.

A few weeks would go by and now this cop was coming to my room. As a matter of fact, sometimes he came twice a day. By this time, they had given me a new cell mate. My cell mate and I didn't really know what to think of this cop. He was just being so cool, a little too cool. All of a sudden this cop started talking about dope. This was right up my alley and also my cell mate's, who was in there for a dope charge, just like me. The cop was telling us that he sells weed. We then say, "What?" He then says, "Yeah, but, I'm out right now." My cell mate then says, "I know where you could get some and then bring some for us." The cop agreed. My cell mate then gave the cop all the info to his girlfriend on the streets. My cell mate told him that he could start getting his dope from her. I was cosigning everything, along with my cell mate.

The cop took all the info down; we had also talked about doing future business, after this one went down. We must have talked to him for another hour and then he left, smiling as usual and more than likely saying to himself, "Dumb ass niggers!"

When he left, we were so excited about making money that we would never get to touch. We couldn't think of anything else but tomorrow, when the cop would bring the dope. My cell mate had already called his girl and prepared her for the cop to come by. We were all smiles thinking about the money we were about to soon be making. We were now into the chips. As a matter of fact, in our minds, we both were going to buy us TVs. We were tired of looking at the walls and not having any entertainment in the room. We were thinking that we were going to be balling again, like we were on the streets again, we could not have been more wrong.

We were so fucking happy talking so much that, we actually got tired from all of this and both of us went to sleep thinking that we would be rolling after tomorrow. We went to sleep thinking that once we woke up, it would be the next day. *In prison, if you got a cop bringing in dope, you got it made.* We thought we had it made, with this type of connection. We talked about how there would be no more stressing about the stuff we didn't have. Now, we would have the money to buy everything we needed. In our opinion, life in prison just got better. While anticipating all the money we were going to make, we never ever anticipated what could go wrong. We didn't consider at all the possibilities of getting caught, or getting more time. We didn't consider much at all about the possibilities of something going wrong, and that's when something did go wrong. We talked so much about making so much money that we both got tired and went to sleep. Soon, the unseen possibilities would become reality!

The only problem was there would be more stress coming and this is the type that would get you another 7 to 14 years in prison. We were fools to believe that we would bring in dope, with the help of this cop. *Again. this is what happens when you allow someone to think for you.*

We hadn't been on the prison yard long enough to figure this cop out. Later that day, there was a big knock at the door, this woke us both up. There was a different cop, pushing two pink sheets of paper, up under the door. These were Department

of Corrections charges, for trying to get the cop to bring drugs into the prison system for which, we could go back downtown through the courts, for new state charges. These papers indicated that we would need to answer these charges very soon. We were still kind of sleepy while reading the charges. We both said out loud, "What the fuck?" There would be no more smiles, for a while. This cop had double-crossed us. This son of a bitch tricked us. "That motherfucker" is all we could say. In reality, we tricked ourselves.

I had been warned about motherfuckers like this, and now I finally got a chance to meet one, up close and personal. *I could be facing more time, for some more stupid shit of mine* is all I could think quietly within my mind. We fell for the banana in the tailpipe, so to speak. I couldn't believe that something like this could get me another 7 to 14 years. Everyday was very stressful, from this point on because, I knew the seriousness of these charges. It was my first court date, while in prison. They pretty much read the new charges to me and my cell mate and asked both of us, "How do you plea?" We both stated, "Not guilty" and then another court date would be set. Once we got back to our cell, my cell mate and I were in major depression mode. "Fuck! We could be going back downtown for new charges," I said and I couldn't help but to think about how this cop played us. He knew we both were new to the prison system. He used this to trap us into making this kind of stupid mistake.

It's almost impossible to go to prison and do your own time. When stupid shit like this happens, you could get caught up into getting more time. If he wouldn't have approached us with this, it's likely that it wouldn't have taken place. This is how many people who just come to prison to serve a short amount of time end up doing many years. They make stupid mistakes, just like this one. They let other people think for them.

A few more weeks would go by. My cell mate now had moved out of my room. I was walking the yard when I saw my former cell mate holding a private conversation with the police. I said to myself, "I hope this fool isn't snitching on me?" This is about the second or third time I saw him talking to the police. The quiet rule in prison is you don't talk to police and you speak when spoken to. So in my mind, this dude was snitching on me. So I said to myself, "It's time to check this fool." After he got through talking to the cop, I sneaked up behind him as he was walking down the sidewalk. I said, "Hey nigga, are you snitching on me?" He then responded, "No man." I then said, "Well, why in the fuck are you always in the police's face?" Once again he said, "I wasn't snitching." I then told him "Nigga, you better not ever snitch on me nigga because you got problems, nigga."

Three more weeks would go by and I was not speaking to my former cell mate anymore. Court dates would come and go. At this point, I didn't know what to think. This was really serious. I didn't have any money for a lawyer on the streets. All of a sudden, later on one evening, I would hear on the loudspeaker "Leary 65798 roll up, roll your shit up." I said

to myself "Damn, where am I going now?" Little did I know, I would be going to a new prison and I would hear of this incident no more.

Rincon Unit, Tucson, Arizona

Now I was on a yard, where I even got more freedom, this was my first real prison yard. What I liked about it more was they had a weight pile, a big one. By this time I was bench pressing 420 pounds. No one on the yard could bench 400. There were a lot of gang members and people who had been busted for dope on the streets on this yard. Even worse, baby fuckers and rapists were there as well.

They all so had the Duct Tape Bandit on the yard. They say he was taking young girls to motel rooms and then duct taping their mouths shut and then sexually abusing them. I anticipated hitting this guy in the head one day when I would realize a few months later that some of the guys that were black and I was hanging out with were rapists too. Then it wouldn't take me long to find out I was in a prison yard that housed the majority of the baby fuckers and rapists in Arizona. Eventually, I would lose the drive to do something to the Duct Tape Bandit. The prison yard was nearly a quarter full of child molesters and rapists.

They just threw me in with the worst. In a sense, this is where I needed to be, because I was a hard nut to crack and I was considered to be one of the worst. Gang members— the Bloods and the Crips—respected strength, so this is where I really started getting my respect. I lived on the weight pile. Usually if you wanted me, this is where you could find me. Since I walked alone, meaning I wasn't affiliated with any gangs, I needed to live at the weight pile.

These guys will try you, so I got my respect by being the strongest on the prison yard. The gangs respected this. By this time, I was running around with 22-inch biceps.

A brother was large. Here the strong prey on the weak, you were either going to be somebody's bitch, or stand up for yourself. Needless to say, there were a bunch of bitches running around on this yard. Greedy D wasn't ever going to be somebody's bitch or punk. So I lifted iron twice a day five to six days a week, daily and indefinitely with no restrictions. At one point I was lifting so much iron, Cops were starting to get intimidated by my size. I was warned by a fellow inmate that, I wouldn't last very long if I keep lifting weights and getting bigger, like I was doing. I took this comment with a grain of salt. He wasn't lying.

What he was telling me was the truth; it just came to be in a strange way. They only locked us down for three times a day here, during count. The rest of the time, we were outside running around. There was a lot of dope on this yard. This is where I smoked my first joint since I had been in prison. This is also when I would start selling weed in prison for the very first time. Once again, I was doing stupid shit. At one point on this yard, I was walking around while going through pat-downs and searches with two ounces of weed in my shorts, for nearly three days. Not thinking about the shit I just got out of at the other yard. I was walking around like I was on the streets. I was walking around being foolish. I had met a bunch of strange fucking characters on this prison yard, some crazy as fuck, but then I realized, they were no different than me, that's why I was there.

I would get my first roommate named Cat. It was strange because at this time, everybody called me "Big Dog." Cat was a pretty big youngster, he respected me and I him. He would lift with me from time to time, on the weight pile. Cat was also the type of guy who would always be into it with somebody, he was a blood. Drama followed Cat, so it would also follow me. I hung out from time to time with both sides, the Crips and the Bloods, it didn't matter to me.

Little did I know it at the time, Cat and I would be cell mates at two more prisons. Cat and I became pretty good friends. We both didn't have much in our rooms so this gave us something in common; so we had to improvise from time to time. Cat and I would bully people from time to time. We took a lot of Inmates Store directly and indirectly. Sometimes we would take it, at the same time the cops were dropping it off. This would be the start of a bunch of bullshit. We were two big guys, so we went around taking and stealing things from people. At this point in time, I had been in prison for nearly a year. The drug flow was almost like being on the streets here. There aren't any drug shortages here. I personally knew this guy who had this cop, a female working in the kitchen, who was the mule. She brought a lot of dope in for this brother. She brought in a quarter-pound of weed for me and my friends.

I would eventually learn that it didn't matter what size a man was, you don't bully any one because, that would be a good way to get some cold steel run up in you. Once that happened, depending on the mercy of your attacker, you could be in big trouble. You would grow to be a peaceful guy, if you survived.

However, there were other ways that the dope was coming in. From time to time you would hear about some one dying at visitation, while trying to bring in heroin, or cocaine, or even worse meth. From what I understood, one guy was out there at visitation drinking sodas, after swallowing several balloons filled with dope. This is a no-no when sneaking drugs into the institution because, the acid in the soda eats away at the balloon while it's in your stomach. According to an eye witness, he died right there on the spot. There were outrageous things that these dudes would be willing to do to get the drugs in, including jeopardizing one's life. This would seem crazy to a normal human being. But for someone who understands addictive behavior, nothing when it comes to getting that drug is off limits, including killing someone.

Sometimes you can tell when the drugs were coming in, because, the heroin addicts would be pacing back and forth in anticipation on someone coming from visitation. The real weight, meaning larger amounts of drugs, came in by the cops; they were the major players.

I would eventually meet this Crip brother named James Brown. James was another crazy man. James had been eyeing this white dude, who had a slim waist and long hair. This white dude was just asking for problems, because he kind of looked like a girl. He also wore tight jeans. He had no hair on his face and he would look good to a twisted motherfucker. James Brown felt immediate attraction for him. After doing years of confinement, one with a weak mind could get confused. Needless to say, James was confused like a motherfucker. I decided long ago that I was not fucking another man in the ass, nor was I letting one suck my penis; this was just out of the question. James had been eyeing this white boy, for at least a couple of weeks. James was doing a ten-year sentence, so his mind was a little distorted. This guy James didn't take another thing into consideration. He could have started a riot by playing this guy too close; however, James wanted some of that ass now. I figured that I was just going to continue building my tee pees late at night, to relieve my tensions. I thought it was like, the lesser of two evils. Every time I thought of sex, I would build my little tent or teepee, or hit a hot shower or whatever it took, other than fucking another man in the rear.

This was my first year, and a long time going without sex, sometimes just the thought of sex would trigger my hand into automatically grabbing my pistol. I thought this was better than looking at some dude's balls hanging, while I was ramming his asshole out.

James came into my cell just after lunch saying to me, "Hey Big Dog, I'm fixing to fuck that white boy." I said to James, "You are a fucking fool man." James then said "Big Dog, that's a fine motherfucker." I seriously didn't think he was serious at the time, but James was very serious, he had the eye of the tiger. Coincidently, this white dude would walk by my cell right at that moment. James saw him and said, "Hey man, come on in here for a minute." The dude came on in like a fool. I was standing up at the time and James was sitting with the white dude, on the bed. James said to him, "You are a pretty motherfucker. Hey, why don't you give me some of that ass." The white dude looked up at James and said "No." The very next thing I knew, James was wrestling with the white dude. He had him in a headlock, trying to take his pants off, and then yelling to me as they both were on the floor tussling.

"Big Dog, take his pants off." I repeated to James man, with a frown on my face, "I'm not taking off his pants." I then said to him, "You got to be fucking crazy." Like I said, James had the eye of the tiger; my man was serious and determined to get him some ass. He just didn't have enough wind. While thinking of the incident I just had been in, over at the other prison, all I could think of at the time was, new charges. "Fuck no, James," I responded again as James continued to ask me to slide his pants down.

While James still had him in a headlock. James was very serious at this time, this brother wanted to fuck, not now, but right now. It was like watching those animals on *Wild Kingdom,* when it's time for sex. This California Crip Brother was crazy and he was tripping. James tried to take his pants down for at least 20 minutes, with no luck. The white guy didn't smoke and he was long winded. Not only this but, if he had gave up and gave James some then, he would have to keep giving James some and anyone else who came around with a hard one. My man James would run out of gas and would be forced to give up in his endeavor. The white guy fought back and was in tears at this time.

To make matters worse, all this shit was going down in my cell. James was a heavy cigarette smoker; he had run out of steam. He was forced to let the white guy go on about his business. This dude left my cell in tears; I then said to James, "Hey man, that was some crazy fucking shit dude."

I had seen a lot of things in my time, but this was at one point humorous and bizarre, all at the same time. You can't get it twisted, this is prison. This type of thing goes on daily inside the prisons. This was only the beginning; it would soon get even crazier.

In 1992, as I said earlier, Cat kept drama around him 24/7 and because, he was my cell mate, he was often the blame for most of the shit that got started in our pod, in my opinion. I will never forget one week after Christmas. They would let food packages come in from the streets. Most of the guys, misfits and fuck ups like me, had burned a lot of bridges and didn't receive anything from the streets. So needless to say, during Christmas time, the stress factor was high. I remember being in our cell when Cat said to me, "These white guys don't share with us, Big Dog." I responded "Yeah man, they only share with their buddies."

Cat then said, "Hey man, when they open this cell, I'm going to take some food from this white boy." I wasn't prepared for what was about to happen next. I thought that Cat would just walk up and take his food box. He had taken it to the next level. Cat walks into the white guy's room, and beat this guy named Jack to a pulp. I thought all he was going to do was just take his food. Cat went in and then closed the cell door behind him and just started beating him.

I had heard a lot of pounding going on, but I never thought this would happen like this. Cat came back to the room with visible anger showing on his face and blood on his fist. "Dog." Cat said, with spoils from the beat down in his hand, "I had to beat him down man." Cat then said with a very mean look on his face, "Dog, I'm tired of these motherfuckers not sharing." Cat had blood running down his knuckles. I immediately went to Jack's room, while looking in; I couldn't believe what I was seeing. This guy Jack was lying on the bed, with blood shooting up like little volcano eruptions. Jack was unconscious and just bleeding.

At this point, I was upset with Cat because, he didn't have to do this to this guy—especially not for the little bit of food that he came back to the room with. This guy would have just given it to Cat. Cat was brutal and a bully, this guy was already afraid of Cat. I didn't like this at all. Next thing we hear over the intercom, "Lockdown, Lockdown, Inmates, Lockdown right now." The guards then came to Jack's room, with a medical assistant and wheeled Jack to the hospital. I would never see this guy Jack ever again. At this time, I felt sorry for this guy because, it didn't take this to get his food from him. Apparently Jack never had a chance. From what I heard, Jack was sitting on the bed and Cat just started pounding him while he was sitting down. This was brutal. This was prison.

The very next thing I knew, our door popped open. It was the guards, and they wanted to see our knuckles. "Leary, show us your knuckles," the guard shouted. "Okay

Cat, show us your knuckles." The guard then asked, "Cat, why do your knuckles have cuts on them?" Cat then gives some lame excuse. The door then closed. Fifteen minutes later, we would here carts rolling down the hallway. I was then saying to Cat, "Hey man, they are coming to get you." I was half right; they came to get me also.

"All right both of you guys, roll up your shit." the guard yelled. I then said to the guard, "What the fuck did I do?" The guard said again, "Leary roll your shit up now." They took us to the hole, which was located on the yard until morning, when we both would talk to the warden. I had never met this guy, but I had heard he was a genuine, asshole.

The very next day, just ten minutes into our conversation, I would find out that the myths circulating about this man were true. "Leary, I know you ordered the fight between Cat and Jack," the warden would then say.

It was almost like either Cat told him this, or he had an informant supplying him with all the info which was false—I never ordered this. I said, "Excuse me, warden," I then said to him, "I resent that remark." The warden then said to his Captain, "Lock Leary's ass down."

I did not order this fight; however, they wanted me off this yard and this was their chance. I was warned that I was getting too big on this yard and I would not last.

By this time I had won the weight lifting competitions there and I had got a lot of respect from the gangs which were plentiful. Little did I know they had a special place for fuck ups like me and Cat? Now it was time to do some hard time, it was time for solitary confinement. It was time to get our minds right.

Central Detention Unit,
24-Hour Lockdown

Just over a year had come to pass and now I was in solitary confinement. There was no more running around nearly all day. Now it was time to think about why I was there in the first place. Cat and I were once again cell mates and the stress factor was so high that it was almost popping off the Richter scale.

By this time, all my old friends were history. Everyone had moved on and changed their phone numbers. I was alone, or so I thought. Once again, it was time for prayer. I just couldn't see it at this time, because of all the negativity that surrounded me. *God would soon send me a sign.*

I had been praying off and on during this year in prison. Now it was time for me to start praying some more because, it was hard and to be honest, I couldn't handle it and that's just keeping it real. At C.D.U., it was hell. Any time you came out of your room, you were placed in handcuffs. You went nowhere without them, even to the shower. If you got no love from the streets, it only intensified the pain of being there. Cat and I had no entertainment in our cell, so we were basically looking at the walls. During the summertime, we sweated like dogs in these cells and maybe that's what we were. I remember a lot of times sitting by the vent, with my shirt off and nothing but sweat, pouring down my whole body while feeling somewhat dehydrated, while Cat would be sweating by the bunk waiting for his chance to sit by the vent. At times, when I would see the guard coming by, I would say to the guard, "Hey man, its fucking hot in here." The guard would respond, "There's nothing we can do about it." Meaning basically, this was part of your punishment, live with it. In reality we made this bed, so we had to live in it.

I didn't order the fight; however, I had done so much wrong in my life, there were still more dues to be paid.

The punishment was also in the meal, you got smaller portions here. This place was a small prison within a prison. They basically did what they wanted there. Here, there were no holds barred. Here, they also had the permission to kick the living shit out of you. Trust me some of us got our asses kicked. Some of us just wouldn't learn. While in solitary confinement, you get a chance to focus on what got you here. When you are doing so much time, locked down 24 hours, it can get mentally weird. I watched some guys lose their mind after being in lockdown in solitary confinement for over a year. Some would throw urine and feces at some of the cops, or smear it on themselves, or smear it on their cell windows. I guess when you are treated like an animal, you will respond like one. Others would break down and cry. Needless to say, I cried myself.

At this point in my life, it was time to be a man, and accept total responsibility for all the things that I had done. No matter what I have done; I would never stop praying to God for a way out, because this is what my mother taught me to do. God would soon send two angels. One would be Tom, who owned a stereo business, he had heard that I was locked down and came to my aid. This man sent me everything I needed, while in prison. He didn't owe me a dime. Tom would never leave my side, through the remainder of the five-year sentence. There's no doubt, he was a godsend.

He also sent this good-hearted woman named Parmella, who would often say that God was telling her to help me and that she was required by Him to give me money once a month. I didn't believe this then; however, I believe this now. *This is how God's work is done.* I would spend one year here at C.D.U. caged up like some animal. For the things that I have done, this cage fit perfectly. I had to be taken to the lowest of lows. I needed to be belittled and dehumanized to see the light.

Cimarron Prison 1992

I had heard about this place many times before, but now I was there waiting at the front gates to be taken through the doors. This was a place to test your fighting skills, whether real or imaginary. All that shit about what you thank you could do and how bad you were, now it was time to prove it. Nobody I knew wanted to be there, because there was always someone getting hurt. Nearly everybody had a shank, or some sharp instrument.

Inmates were locked down for twenty-two and a half hours, every day. Every day was basically the same there, stressful. They had guards that stood on towers with their guns visibly seen. They also had orders to shoot. When the doors racked opened in your pod for chow, which was served in a building about one hundred yards walking distance, then this is when most of the shit would go down that couldn't get solved while on the weight pile the previous day. I would see many get their ass broken off.

From time to time, I would see a body bag being taken out of this place. Every chance I got, I lifted weights and water bags in my cell. I knew because I was hardheaded, shit would soon come to my door. My mother used to complain about me being hardheaded back in the days. Indeed, this is the place to have a lot of different behaviors dealt with, so I kept my physique strong and muscular. Cimarron was infamous for the gangs and stabbings.

There, you had more Crips than Bloods, you also had your Aryan Brothers and your Mexican Mafia. This alone would

keep shit going. There were all kinds of drugs there. Heroin
was plentiful as well as meth, cocaine and weed. Inmates and
cops brought the drugs in, that's for sure. Here is where I sold
a lot of weed. It was here where I got my first cop to bring
in dope for me and my cell mate. My cell mate brought in a
good share of the dope too. Cimarron Unit was a real fucked
up place to be, but for me it was about to be all good. At least,
that's what I thought?

After going through the dehumanization process of
looking up my ass by some cop, we were given blankets and
then escorted to our cells. This is where I would meet my first
cell mate, Pete. Once his door racked open, you could see the
fear on his face. Pete was only about maybe 175 pounds.

Once he had seen how swollen I was, with large arms
hanging out of the orange jumpsuit that I was forced to
wear, during transport, his next words after introducing
himself was, "Man you are not a homosexual, are you?" I
started to fuck with him, when I told him in so many words,
"I don't like shit on my dick." I could see on his face, a
sigh of relief. Pete and I would later get to be good friends.
Pete later that week would tell me about how the drugs
came in and that he brought in a lot himself, with the help
of his girlfriend. Pete was in prison for something he did
that required him to do seven years; however, just two years
prior, Pete had been given more time for bringing in drugs
through visitation and was sentenced to another seven
years. Pete schooled me on being locked down and bringing in dope. This is how it worked.

Pete would arrange from a phone call to have his girl bring
the dope in her womb. Once she would get to visitation area
with the inmate, she would then go to the restroom. Once
there, she would retrieve the balloon lodged in her womb, then
go back out to the visitation area, and then while the guard

wasn't looking, make the switch. Then, Pete would go back into the restroom, where he would take that same balloon and lodge it up his ass. This process took a lot of balls and teetered around stupidity to get the drugs in; however, this is just one way that the drugs came in.

Pete would then come back to the cell, where a bunch of guys that knew him would stand waiting anxiously to get high. Needless to say, I was one of these guys. Pete would come back to the cell and then the guards would buzz him in through the doors. Pete was ingenious, so to speak. Pete would shit the balloon out, while I would be in the cell with him. This part was nasty. The whole cell would always during this time smell like pure shit. I don't care how much cologne we would sometimes spray, it would just smell like sweet shit.

Being locked in this room, only intensified this process. Once Pete recovered the balloon and washed it off, the smell would die down a little bit, but the aroma would hang in the air. Pete's girl, only bought him the bum ass weed. Once we got this shit and some rolling papers and smoked the first joint, the process of bringing the dope in, would be forgotten. It would just be a formality. Pete was a bad man, in my opinion, because, I didn't have the balls to do this. This indeed took big balls because if they caught you doing this, as Pete had explained, your ass is finished. Pete had been caught doing this once already and wasn't scared to do this again. He was tough or crazy, you make the call.

Pete brought in dope twice a month. Pete kept big store and money on his books. Just like when a nigga is making money, you then have your banana-eating niggas standing on the corner talking about how I don't like that shit. We are going to have to drop dime on them niggas.

I Had Just Snagged My First Mule, He Was a Cop

I had just gotten a job doing laundry in our pod. I didn't like washing clothes, especially, a motherfuckers underwear; however, there was a method to the madness. This gave me ample time out of my cell to sell the drugs that Pete was bringing in. Also, if one of these niggas ever got out of line, I could tell them about their shitty asses. So when I would go around delivering the laundry, I would also deliver my weed. It was at this time, a few cops started liking me because a brother was large and cool in their opinion, or so they thought? It was at this point this one Mexican cop, would always call me Big Leary and ask about my weight training plan. He was just being too cool with me. He was coming to our cell every day, for a two-week period. We would be sitting there, then all of sudden, the door would pop open and it would be him, smiling as usual. This cop was just being too cool, so now it was time for Greedy D to come to the surface. Soon as the cop would come into our cell that day, I would say to him, "Hey man, are you our friend or what because, you keep coming in our room man?" I then said, "You are not trying to bust us, are you?" "He then said, "No man, I just like you guys." I then said to him "Man, you got any weed man?" He then surprisingly said, "Yeah, but not on me, I got a joint in the car." I then said to him, "Hey man, could you bring me some weed tomorrow?" He said "Yeah," and after talking for another few minutes, he left. Pete and I begin to talk about what happened over at Ryening Unit, when the cop tricked me. To be honest, I didn't know if the cop would be turning us in for the conversation that we just had.

I had to try him because, the number-one rule is you don't talk to the cops unless you are spoken to first. When I went to sleep that night, I couldn't help but to wonder, what the next day would bring. When the next day came, we knew this cop would work our pod, that evening. We watched out our cell window, for the guard's shift to change. We started smiling when he came into our pod and then to our cell. My heart was racing in my chest when the cop reached in to both boots and pulled out two bags of skunk bud weed. Having an ounce each of skunk bud in prison was like having a pound of weed on the streets. Man, I couldn't believe what had just taken place! In my mind, we had just hit the motherload.

A cop just brought me marijuana in prison. I kept thinking in my mind that I had made it. Next thing you know, not only was the cop bringing in weed when he saw us, but he was also bringing in cocaine for my cell mate, Pete. I didn't want any of this stuff, so I let Pete handle that. I wasn't strong mentally enough to carry this stuff around at the time. Pete was the man; he would carry this stuff around and most people wouldn't even know it. It was real hard to believe that I had it going on like this. My cell mate was bringing in weed, along with this cop. At one point, we had too much dope in our cell. Since money couldn't change hands in the joint, I sent a lot of money to the streets to get washed and sent back to me. As in any good thing, there are always some fools that will come along and fuck things up for you.

After about a four-week period, other inmates were starting to take notice of how cool the cop was, and just like some bitch niggas, it started circulating that we could be giving up information, never ever realizing that, this is how they got their drugs. Man, the very next thing you knew Pete was just doing a few lines of cocaine in the room on some plastic piece of paper. We had just smoked a joint, when Pete put the weed back in the balloon, back in the bank, back basically in his ass. He called it the bank, I called it his ass.

That's basically what he did, Pete would take it out of his ass, just what he was going to smoke that day; the rest he would put back into the balloon, and he would stick it back up his ass. Pete would go out and play basketball with an ounce of dope in his ass and nobody would know it. Pete was a bad man.

All of a sudden one day while in our cell, about a half hour after smoking a fat joint, our door popped open—it was the cops, real ones. Before they could get in the cell, Pete had dumped the plastic clear paper with the dope on it in the toilet; he tried to flush it, but it didn't flush. The cops rushed us; three of them searched the room upside down. One cop even looked in the toilet, where Pete had put the rest of the cocaine—it wasn't much. After the cops searched for about a half hour, they then let us back in the room. Not before strip searching us of course, they wanted to see assholes and elbows.

Once we got back into the room, we realized that these bitch niggas was hating on us, that's when Pete looked down and realized that the cocaine was still on the plastic paper floating on the water. Pete then picked it up carefully out of the water and started snorting more lines after they rushed us. If I hadn't seen this for myself, I wouldn't have believed it.

In every prison, the warden has his snitches. However, there would be other snitches that would come along who wouldn't necessarily work for the warden. They just were other inmates, the hating type that would snitch, just so you didn't excel.

This was the first time we had been bum rushed for drugs. Things would get even harder, when the Mexican Mafia found out that we had a Mexican Cop bringing us in dope. After about one month that the cop worked for me and Pete, he just cut us off. He would not even speak to us again. Later, I realized that now the Mexican Mafia had him. After about a month of working with them, he quit, just like that. Nobody would ever see him again. They must have threatened him, because, I saw this cop talking to one of their leaders outside his door for at least a half hour or so. I figured that they must have pumped fear in him, because they were good at that and they didn't play. When the Mexican Mafia told their people something, they seldom had to repeat themselves. They put fear into people on the yard.

The main mafia leader at Cimarron would receive whole sacks of store from other inmates. You could only shop at the store once a week; guys would drop off their whole sack at his door every week like clockwork. Some guys never had store for themselves. They were paying homage to this guy. You either did what you were told, or suffered the consequences and most people would just do what they were told, end of story.

It was the summer of 1992, at Cimarron Prison; things were starting to get really bad. This was the first time anyone had asked me to kill someone. This nigga who was doing a 25-year bid for murder, was also one of the members of a black gang. While on the weight pile, he would say to me, "Hey, Big Dog, I want you to kill someone for me." I said, "What nigga?" He again said, "I want you to kill someone for me." I told him, "Look here nigga, I'm not killing anyone, I got six years and six years only, nigga, I'm going home." He didn't press the issue and thankfully, it didn't go any farther than that. If this had been a Mexican Mafia, asking their people to do this, it would have been done. It would have had to have been carried out, or that person would have been shanked. I respected them, because they didn't play.

One of the Mexican Mafia members had just overdosed in his cell. I will never forget seeing his body being taken out in a black bag. I remembered him well, because we had words over at C.D.U., I had to tell him to fuck himself. We were supposed to get our scrap on, once we got to Cimarron; however; we would never be put in the same pod. His body was now being taken out of his cell. According to his cell mate, he was already dead when he woke up that morning from a heroin overdose.

I believe another guy had also overdosed and was taken to the hospital a short time after this. Warden Mouse was fed up with the drugs and ordered the yard locked down and searched for a week. Nobody got visits, and no dope came in. Warden Mouse was also a genuine son of a bitch. There were also more people getting jumped, or stabbed, almost weekly. When there weren't any drugs on the yard, in my opinion, tempers flaired, inmates went the fuck off. They have to keep everyone in lockdown. He kept locking down the yard, more and more and not allowing visits. Nobody could get their dope in. Even the cops were scared to bring dope in, so none came in.

The cops were now throwing surprise searches and doing a lot more random searches in our cell and other cells without notice. They started doing sneaky searches. They would just run in from outside and go straight to your room and begin searching; this would also include us being strip-searched. This type of thing went on daily. Warden Mouse was determined to stop the flow of drugs inside his institution. Also we were forced to be in our room 24 hours a day, during this time Warden Mouse was fighting a losing battle. However, I would give him an E for the effort. It's hard to stop the flow of drugs inside any institution, especially if it's your own employees lending a helping hand in the drug trade.

I was getting sick of this shit and this warden, so what I tried to do was send a loud and clear message to him, by organizing a work stoppage. Inmates do all the work in prison so, if it's a work stoppage, that meant the cops had to get off their lazy asses and do the work, and they didn't like that.

I tried very hard to organize everyone and failed. It was a losing battle, just like Warden Mouse and his battle to stop the drug trade. There's no unity within the races in Prison, none. Every day it seemed like this warden was doing shit to upset me. I had just started to get visits, for the first time in my sentence when they were suspended. I knew he was trying to stop the flow of drugs. At the same time, I was trying to get more visits that just had begun. So Warden Mouse and I would, so to say, bump heads. If there were unity in the prisons, the inmates could bring just about every prison to its knees, or put it this way, the prisons would have some very serious problems that they are totally not prepared for.

So I thought a personal kite to this asshole would make a difference. So I wrote it with my left hand, so that they couldn't figure out who wrote it and then dropped it in the box, addressed to Warden Mouse. It read,

*"YOU SON OF A BITCH, WHEN WE SEE YOU
ON THE YARD, WE ARE GOING TO SHANK YOU."*

What the hell did I do this for? This would get an overwhelming response. Warden Mouse locked down the entire yard. He wanted all assholes and elbows showing.

These cops turned this whole prison inside out, something that I had never anticipated, when sending this letter to him. Everyone lost their visits again, no drugs came in and inmates were pissed. At this point, I didn't know what else to do to put fear in Warden Mouse; however, he would never walk the yard with less than three cops surrounding him at all times. So in a sense the letter worked, because he was afraid and I did that to him. I pumped fear into Warden Mouse. I wanted him to fear being hurt, just like I feared losing my visits.

Pete's prison score dropped and he would be sent to another yard where his life would soon change for the worse. I would have a few different cell mates, when the Department of Corrections tried to desegregate us; they tried to put two different races in one room. This was something the Department of Corrections had figured out that they would do probably in one day, to save space—never anticipating the anger it would cause between the races. Each race vowed to never live in a cell with each other. I would see a few guys of different races try to go into the cell in violation of inmate rules, of a different race living with each other and get that ass stumped. This went on for at least one month, when the Department of Corrections figured out that they were causing more harm than good and dropped their failed policy altogether.

All of a sudden, I was in the room without a cell mate when the doors would pop open and Cat would come walking into the room. I said, "I don't believe it, what's up, Cat?" He then said, "What's up, Dog?" He said, "I told you that I was going to be seeing you again." I smiled in happiness to see him again. This smile would soon turn into pain. Like I said at Rincon Prison, where ever Cat went, drama followed. It wouldn't take long for drama to come.

At Cimarron, there were more Crips than Bloods and Cat just so happened was a Blood that was sent into a pod full of Crips. A brother was large, so I got respect from both sides. A few members of the Crips had informed me that they wanted to get with Cat. I told them that they would have to fight me to. Cat was a scrapper no doubt, however, this was the first time I had ever seen fear on Cat's face. Cat was outnumbered, and when it came to getting your ass whipped by a gang, you would probably be fighting more than one after all—this is how they do it.

Cat was a big youngster who always walked around with his chest out; however, this time he had to eat crow. Everywhere I went in the pod during recreation, Cat was on my heels. He was outnumbered and the only friend he had was me. However, Cat was soon nearly knocked out in the Chow Hall. Like I said, this is where a lot of business gets taken care of, on the way to the Chow Hall. It just so happened that, Cat made it inside. This one nigga went upside Cat's dome; they say he beat the shit out of Cat.

What had actually happened was Cat got some of what he dished out over at Rincon. Shit has a way of coming back at you. He got caught talking shit, while sitting down. This is a big no-no. As a matter of fact, Cat was walking around with one of his headlights out, meaning a black eye. He was then asking me, what I think he should do for what had just happened to him? For anybody else, it would be obvious what he should do. I told him what you mean what should you do, you just got your ass kicked. You should fight him again. It was at this moment, when I realized that Cat wasn't as tough as he portrayed; he was afraid and trying to make everyone believe that he was tough. His chest wasn't sticking out as before and it was obvious that Cat didn't want anymore of that brother.

They would move Cat to the hole eventually and my score would drop, which means, I could be sent to another prison. I tried unsuccessfully to be moved to Santa Rita Prison, which was a lower custody yard, next door. My prison counselor informed me that I couldn't go there. I said, "Why not?" she said, "I'm not at liberty to discuss that with you."

I said, "What? You mean to tell me that I can't go to Santa Rita that's just next door?" She then repeated herself, kind of angrily, "I can't discuss this with you, I'm sorry." That same day, I would get another cell mate who would come from Santa Rita Prison. After talking for a while that day, trying to get to know each other, he mentioned out of the blue that this brother named Rolo was on that yard. That's when I jumped up off my bunk and described Rolo to him, when he said, "Yep, that's that bitch." I then told him, "That's the bitch that got me here and I want his blood." He then told me, "Other brother's were fucking him in the ass on that yard. They turned him into a bitch." I responded, "That shouldn't have been hard for them to do."

I would soon hear the words over the intercom, "Leary 65798 roll up" a week later. I had served my time at Cimarron. I had been thrown in a pot with the worst and survived, so now it was time to get to someplace where I could relax and do the rest of my time. Wrong. I would soon realize once again, that this was prison and there was no relaxing. You got to be on your guard at all times. This was prison where, the strong preyed on the weak. To relax is just a want, there's a genuine need to survive.

Perryville Prison 1993

Once I had gotten on the bus headed to Perryville, I would see a face that I would not expect to see. Cowboy was also shackled down on the bus; I couldn't believe my eyes. I immediately walked over to him and said "Cowboy, what the hell are you doing on this bus?" Cowboy then explained when he said, "Cowboy, shortly right after you got caught and went to prison, the cops then raided my house and found 300

pounds of pot." He then said, "Just like you, some rat bas-
tard set me up." I then said to him "Man, that's fucked up
man." We then talked for a few more minutes, when I had to
take my seat at the insistence of the guard.

I then said to Cowboy, "We will talk more, once we hit
the yard." Of all people, I never thought Cowboy would be
on the same bus with me headed to Perryville. Soon as I hit
the yard, I heard that they had just come off lockdown, even
worse they had just busted Pete again, for bringing in weed
from visitation. I heard they might have gotten his girl also.
This one inmate explained how it all went down; he said,
"Overhead in the bathrooms they installed Cameras inside the
vent, so they can see inmates when they are on the toilet in
the bathroom." He then said, "Pete had gone through the strip
down while at visitation, when the cop noticed a piece of a
balloon hanging out Pete's ass." He said, "Pete then tried to
run across the yard when he was tackled out in the field by
three cops. They then shackled him up like a dog."

He said they then, "taped around his waist with duct tape
and then taped his pants legs, so he couldn't shit it out, on
the way to the shit room." This is a room where they hand-
cuff you to a chair, for three straight days buck naked, until
you shit out the contraband into a bucket. This bucket is
placed under the hole that is cut out into the chair.

In three days on this chair buck naked, anyone will want
to shit, just to get off of the chair. We were hoarded off the
bus, into this big building. By this time we knew the routine,
drop your pants spread those cheeks. I just couldn't get used
to this shit. I didn't enjoy another man looking up my ass. I
felt this was degrading and dehumanizing, however; this is
what I lowered myself to. This is where they kept all the new
inmates, for a forty-five day period. We were mixed in with
all kinds of races of people in this building. Finally, I was

close to home after three years and Cowboy and I started talking more. I asked Cowboy could he get some pot in? He said, "Maybe, however, the Mexican Mafia don't want me talking to you anymore." I then said to him, "Just tell them that we knew each other from the streets." He then said, "They don't care about that shit, Cowboy."

The very next thing I would notice later on that day was, the cops would come in and roll all of Cowboy's stuff up. Cowboy wasn't anywhere to be seen. I'm saying in my mind, "What the fuck?" I would later find out that, Cowboy went to protective custody. I would soon lose respect for Cowboy; this was the dude that, got me hooked on cocaine, someone that I admired as a kid. This was the guy who I admired and respected and I thought was bad. Now Cowboy was in protective custody. I soon would see the guards walking Cowboy to meds. When you are in P.C. you go everywhere chained up and with at least two cops. They put you in the bright orange jump suits and they put you in cells sometimes with three or more.

When it's a hundred and twenty degrees outside, it's even hotter inside the small cells, with three people and to top it all off, there's only two beds. So usually someone has to sleep with their mattress on the floor next to the toilet. When somebody has to take a shit, the other two suffer. protective custody is no joke; sometimes you are better off fighting.

Cowboy was an old number, meaning he had been here before. The rule is you never let anyone P.C. you up, unless you are a bitch. The rule is you're supposed to hit the biggest one in the mouth, the one that's starting all the shit. Even if you get your ass stumped and most likely you would, you would save face on the yard. Cowboy knew the rules. Even if the guy kicks the living shit out of you, he would respect you later. So to just voluntarily go to P.C. was unacceptable in my opinion—Cowboy had turned bitch.

That evening I needed to use the phone to try and schedule a visit, when I noticed the guy in front of me on the phone. He was coughing all over the phone and sneezing in the air. I didn't think much of this, as he handed me the phone, once he was done. I had called Parmella to come and visit me. As I hung up the phone with her, I immediately became sick, like the guy who had just gotten off the phone. Even worse, after trying to take all kinds of medications I could find, I would later suffer a stroke.

They called it Bell's Palsy. One side of my face just fell and it was numb. I looked deformed, as I looked in the mirror. I felt weird, I then went to the guard station, where I was taken from there to the medical complex, when they found the time to take me, of course. Once I had gotten there, they gave me steroids to take daily, for the next few days. I couldn't talk, my voice was slurred. To make things worse, I looked deformed. I looked crazy. Every day I looked in the mirror, I begged the mighty God saying, "Please don't let me stay like this."

Three more weeks would pass and it was time for me to be moved to a pod. These pods at Perryville housed approximately 60 inmates. This was a medium security yard where your room doors actually faced outside. Once the doors were unlocked by the guards, you were outside, with the other 60 inmates. Don't get it confused, this was prison; shit went on here daily. Nearly every Friday night, the dust flew up on the side of the pod, when someone didn't pay their dope bill, or when someone needed attitude adjustment. Usually when someone didn't pay their bill, interest was usually taken out of someone's ass and they still had to pay.

The clanging of weights hitting the ground every day was the scene.The drugs, the bitches and the gangs were fluent here. This place reminds me of Death Valley. As you look at it while shackled down in the bus from the highway, it's located in the middle of the desert. It just looks so dry and lonely. For someone who didn't have a family, this is exactly what it is. The cops and inmates brought in the dope.

I personally knew one of the cops, who was bringing in the weed because I wanted him to bring some in for me. He was bringing so much dope in for everybody else that, I had to take a number. He never would get around to me. There was never a shortage of drugs there. Every weekend the dope came in from the inmates. The cops would bring it in, during the week day and at any given time. At this time, cops weren't searched before starting their jobs.

I was immediately attracted to the weight pile. You have to remember, the only things that brothers respected in there was size. I was large, so I got most respect. Riots would start over the stupidest shit. I have to admit it didn't take long for the shit to get started. I wouldn't be on the yard for more then three months when the first riot would take place.

The police were able to get a grip on it, before a lot of inmates got hurt; however, it was my understanding that someone got hit in the head with a bat. The whites outnumbered us by at least 3 to 1 and the Mexicans had us by 4 to 1. However, the blacks had the muscle, because we had been hitting those weights, but we had no choice: there were just too many of them.

Often, the whites and the Mexicans would team up against the blacks. This is how the Department of Corrections kept the Inmate numbers on each yard. So usually when there was a riot, it was the blacks against somebody. Like almost always, it's some stupid shit that gets it started. For example this one hoe-man liked this one white inmate, now the hoe-man is running around with a black inmate. Now somehow or another, it became a fight between the races. Sometimes stuff started from stupid shit like this.

Personal Observation

In prison, the stress factor remains extremely high at all times. This is why the dope will always come in. It's my belief that the police know this is the only way to keep the prison's inmate population calm. The drugs have to keep coming in. First, they all appear to operate, with not enough staff. When there's a riot jumping off, some cops run faster than the inmates do, for safety. If there isn't any dope on the yard, there is no way to keep the peace. The cops couldn't keep control of the prison. This is why the dope will always come in to the prison system. Cops along with the inmates, will always be the instruments, to bring dope into the prisons. This is the way it's been and this is the way it will continue.

The prison system is a homosexual breeding ground, where many women and men go in heterosexual and come out homosexual. I have personally seen both sexes come out of the prison system transformed, or should I say twisted. You have to be stronger than you could ever think, to do a ten-year sentence and not come home with some discrepancies of your moral character. As one female put it, before entering the prison system, "I'm Strictly Dickly"; once returned to society, she loved the taste of another woman. I knew of men, who were locked up, who fanta-sized of ramming another man's back side out. Because of years of being dehumanized, no one could tell them any different. After doing years of confinement and being dehumanized and animalized, one's thinking could get twisted especially, if he or she is weak-minded to begin with. There's got to be something wrong with the system. Change is mandatory.

At Perryville, the summers are so brutal. Your cells are cooled by swamp coolers. When temperatures reached 115 degrees, the coolers didn't work and you sweated like a dog outside and inside of your cell. Indeed some of us were dogs, in my opinion. Also some of us were destined to fail from birth, in my experience. When I was young, I was hated for just being black. So somehow or another, this had to play some role in my opinion as to why I was here. Nonetheless, I was there and this was real and I had to deal with this shit.

All the crying in the beginning from losing all I had was over. I had to man up and accept the cards, which were being dealt to me.

For the most part of it, I felt I deserved everything that I had coming to me. So when shit got hard in here at this point, I would think about that pregnant woman that I had sold my dope to and the families that I helped to destroy. In the summers, when the temperature went up, so did the stress factor. There was always some shit going on. If it was 115 degrees outside, then it had to be 125 degrees in your cell. Sometimes, you would hear cell mates go at it, beating each other down, in their cells. The guards would usually not enter their cell, at this time. What they would do was to open up the trapdoor, which was a small opening in the door in which, if the yard was on lockdown. This is how, they would put food trays through the hole. This is also where they would shoot pepper spray. Believe it or not, you could kill a person like this. Once they shot the pepper spray in the room, they would wait about 5 to 10 minutes before opening the door. It only takes

Fort Grant   1995

a second for the pepper spray to work. Within seconds, both inmates would be fighting to breathe and begging the guards to open the door. The guards would usually take their time to do so, while almost allowing the inmates to die from suffocation. I watched a few nearly pass out from this procedure. I was tired of being here; however, I had to do this and there would be no one that could bring comfort to me but God.

Almost every night, there would also be the dreams of using cocaine and nightmares seeing the police raid my house. The sound of hearing keys opening and closing of doors all night long would be heard in my sleep. Here, you got no rest. It was here, that no one was above the horrors of being in prison. All of a sudden, I begin to get most of the movement back into the right side of my face, from the stroke that I had a year prior. "God was indeed answering my many prayers; however, I was still disobedient to his will. Then one day, I would hear the words that my ears would yearn to hear. "Leary 65798 roll it up."

Finally, the day would come to where I would no longer see the insides of that place again. My score had dropped and I would soon only have a year and a half to go. I was so happy to be going to a minimum security yard. Not only this, but I was heading to a place that was a lot cooler. I couldn't wait to get there. I was happy going around telling everybody that I was cool with that, Greedy D is out of this fucked up place. Everyone I had talked to got a chance to witness the smile that was on my face when I told them see you'all however, this smile was only temporary. As usual, this was prison, there's nothing to be happy about in there. I would soon find out that, I had some more dues to pay. The things that I did many of years ago while on the streets had not been forgotten.

The great State of Arizona had not forgotten about me, even though I had been in prison for four and a half years. Shock and awe was coming and mental pain and anguish came with it. The state considered me a threat and had adopted some surprising plans.

Even worse, I would have a brush with death, which would make any one, send out an emergency call to God. When you believe in your heart that it's over, it would soften up the most hardened of hearts, it softened up minds. "God, please," is all I remembered repeating, as I was being flown out of the prison by helicopter.

Fort Grant Prison 1995

Here, more than enough from every race, was strung out on heroin, this drug came in sometimes daily and weekly. May God continue to bless the soul of "Joey," a friend, who died tragically, from a drug overdose, upon being discharged from this prison, which is what I was told by his daughter. From time to time, I would see Joey on the yard walking around so fucked up that sometimes he wouldn't notice me as he passed by. I would say to him "Joey man, what's up dude, you are all fucked up?" He would say "D, I know ... fuck." I would then say to him, "Be careful, dude," while shaking my head in disbelief. The cops wouldn't have the power to control the flow of drugs inside this institution. As a matter of fact, they were part of the problem because, they were the ones also bringing in the drugs.

There was more heroin on this yard than I had ever seen on any yard. It's my personal belief that, the prison system is indirectly responsible for the death of my good friend Joey because, these cops were also the one bringing in the heroin. The prison system should bear some of the blame, for my friend Joey dying.

It's been over ten years since I've seen the insides of a prison and I'm willing to bet today that drugs are still plentiful inside nearly every prison in Arizona. Drugs will never leave the prison system.

These people took on the responsibility for him, meaning the prison system. They incarcerated him. So, they basically took on the role to change him and to reform him. This is why

they call it the *Department of Corrections.* If it had been left
up to them, I would be dead as well. They simply didn't give
a fuck in prison. This guy Joey walked around the prison yard,
at least two days out of the week, so fucked up and out of his
mind, and not one of the guards cared, or was willing to care,
about Joey. How can someone stagger up and down the prison
yard, at least two days out of the week, with cops watching
and nothing happens. I can tell you, you have to be also directly
involved, in the distribution of the drugs, in my opinion.

Trust me. He was at a point in his life where he was
screaming out for help, silently. Someone should have noticed
especially on a controlled yard. It's my opinion that they failed
Joey and his family. The sad thing about this is that at this
time, Joey was somewhere around 23 years old. Trust me
when I say Joey came from a respectful family and they are
very successful today. He had his family's support, he just
didn't have the support of the prison system, which has not
taken any responsibility for this tragedy. From my understanding, Joey didn't start doing heroin, until he got to Fort Grant.

As on any prison yard, you have to stay ready for any shit
to go down. I ran and worked out at least five days a week.
If you stay ready you never had to get ready, was my theory,
so I kept ready. One of my biggest weaknesses was, I would
go to bed early at night; this is when a lot of shit went down
on the yard. I just couldn't keep my eyes open, when the sun
had gone down. The yard didn't close until 9:30 a.m. and I
was usually in the room by 7 pm. I was awoken one evening
when I was told that some of the youngsters were bullying
and beating up some of the older inmates. They were taking
their food and other belongings. So it was time for those
youngsters to be put into their proper places. I then gathered
up a few of my older inmate buddies and we went on an ass
kicking spree basically. I will never forget that morning

when they were laughing out loud about what they did that following night, as they were gathered up. It was hailing that morning, when I yelled out to them as it was raining. I yelled at them saying, "Before nightfall, all of your asses will be kicked." Most started laughing in disbelief; they didn't believe me. It was somewhere around eight of them. To set an example, I caught one of them behind one of the dorms, who tried to run when he noticed the size of my army.

We were around 10 deep and swollen. I put work on him personally. When I caught him, I started out by kicking him in his ass and then punched him hard in his chest and stomach. When I was done, he wanted to change his ways. He respected older people, after this. We caught another hiding in the shower, his eyes were extremely large when we opened up the shower curtain. His first words were please; however, at this time he needed to be taught a lesson. So we then punched and kick the shit out of him.

He also was reformed at that point. For some time, those youngsters had been getting out of hand. Someone had to help them with getting their minds back right. They didn't believe that I was coming to get in their ass because, it was dark outside this whole day and it was raining and hailing. Most took my treat lightly and without merit. When those doors opened in their dorms and they saw the size of my Army, they went into immediate repentance. Indeed, they were forgiven, but only after the ass whipping that followed.

I didn't live up to my promise, which was to beat all of them down by nightfall. It actually took till that next morning to get to the last one. By this time the cops were aware of what was taking place, but they didn't give a fuck. Not only this but, I helped a lot of them with their jobs, by doing this. We caught the last one in church, when I opened the doors, he was praying. Needless to say, I also apologized to the Lord as I walked in and said to him, "Hey, you know you got to come outside, at one point or another." I then told him, "You might as well get it over with. Your boys have."

I promised him that we weren't going to seriously hurt him, but we just wanted to teach him a lesson. After about five minutes, he came outside the church and we just lifted him off his feet and into the air and carried him to his beat down destination. I did as I promised, I beat the shit out of him, as did my buddies and believe it or not, he turned out to be a good youngster after that. After any war, you make the other live by your rules. It was my decree that these youngsters weren't allowed to gather in fours anymore, only three to a crowd. That if I saw them gathering into a crowd of four or more, I would consider it an act of war and the same thing would happen again. Well, we never had any more problems from the youngsters. They turned out to be pretty cool. Later on however, there would be another fight coming and I wouldn't be prepared for this one either. The only difference was, this one was for my life.

I started running a two for one store, on the yard. From this, I started to make a little money, or should I say store. What I would do was, if any one wanted a bag of chips, candy or a soda or any other food item in my illegal store, they would have to bring two, for every one they took. Within weeks, I had a store, almost as big as the one the cops were running in a building for the inmates. The only difference was they also sold hot food and hygiene items. The real store that the cops ran, sold greasy chicken and cheese burgers. No one ever told me that you could die from this, if you ate this nearly every day. Needless to say, I was eating greasy food almost daily. I was eating chicken and cheese burgers and greasy fries almost daily. A combination of this daily is a silent killer. No one told me.

This was also the first prison that I had been in where, I could actually buy this from the store. After about six months of this, I noticed that when I would wake up from sleeping, my heart would be beating extremely fast. I didn't know what was going on, but I knew something wasn't right. I didn't notice, but the combination between the greasy cheeseburgers and the fried chicken and fries was causing me problems.

Every time I ate this combination of food, I began to feel worse. One night, I was experiencing the signs of having a heart attack. I then walked up to the guard station and before I could get there, I began to collapse. The guards noticed and took me to the nurse's office, where they hooked me up to a heart monitoring device, called an EKG. The helicopter was then called in, to fly me to a hospital. Before they had got there, which would be about two hours later, I had to put in an emergency call to God. It appeared to me that the cops weren't really concerned about me, as I was lying there while having difficulty breathing.

When most people are confident that they are going to die, they will make some kind of attempt to contact God and I was no different. I started praying to God to have mercy, although, in my heart, I felt that I deserved none. I can surely tell you today that he is a God full of understanding and mercy because, He answered my prayers. It was also after this incident when my transformation would begin. It was during this time when I thought things couldn't get any worse, but they did, they got much worse.

One month had gone by since I had left the hospital, and I was still suffering from the complication of eating all those greasy foods. I was now taking heart and blood pressure pills all in one and wondering how could I be so healthy looking on the outside and then dealing with heart-related issues on

188 DAVID ALLEN LEARY

the inside. I started attending church on a regular basis, no doubt about it, I was scared. I really thought I was going to die. I was scared to do anything that I thought would cause my heart to beat fast, including exercise. Almost daily, when I woke up in the morning, my heart would beat out of rhythm. I was so scared because of the irregular beats of my heart daily. Now it was time for things to get worse.

One evening I was lying in my bed scared of what tomorrow would bring for my heart. Two cops entered my room saying to me "Leary 65798, roll your stuff up." I asked them, "Where am I going?" They said they didn't know. However, I needed to roll my stuff up now. Early that morning, the bus pulled up in front of the guard's office.

They began chaining everybody up that was scheduled to depart from Fort Grant that morning. Once again, I asked the guards, "Where are they taking me?" One guard responded that I was going to Central Intake Unit and that was all he could say. I couldn't think for the life of me, why I would be going back to Central Intake Unit, on 24th and Van Buren Street. At this time the Department Of Corrections were arresting people, who thought they were going home on new charges; however, they never rearrested me.

When a person thought he was going home that morning, they would arrest you that night and take you to the hole and then explain to you that you have new charges. There was nothing like doing years in prison and thinking you have completed your sentence and then being rearrested that morning for new charges, while expecting to go home. That's a shocker to your system. I've seen many smiles wiped off of faces of inmates who actually thought they were going home. This is what I called cruel and unusual punishment.

I will tell you now, if you don't already know, this is prison and anything goes. It was obvious to me at this time that, there was more to just doing time in prison. There was a psychological mind whipping, one also received while doing time. They didn't take me to the hole, so I just couldn't think of why I was heading back to Central Intake? Once I had arrived there, they still wouldn't tell me, why I was there? Three days later, the sheriffs came to get me and they still wouldn't tell me where I was going. Once we got all the way to the county jail, it was made obvious to me why I was there. I was being indicted for a new yet old charge of selling cocaine. After doing five years of my six-year sentence, I was being indicted, for a new old charge. Something that they could have stacked on my sentence years ago, when I originally got sentenced.

They had just un-sealed this new indictment and now I was back at the county jail, answering to these charges. I just couldn't believe it; these people knew that I had already done five years, and that I only had one year to go. "Why would they do this to me?" is all I could think. This only made the heart problem I was having worse.

Maricopa County Jail, 1995

I never thought I would ever call prison my home. However, this was where I had rather been, right about then. I was heading back through the horse shoe in the county jail. This was something I hated; in my opinion, this was the worst part about going to jail in Arizona: having to go back through the horse shoe, which was a motherfucker. None the less, I had earned a straight shot through there. It took three days to make it through the horse shoe before I was sent up stairs to finally a mattress. No more sleeping on the iron beds downstairs. No

more smell of piss. Finally some peace, once I get to my cell.
Wrong. Peace is something that I would never have.

While walking through the hallway, while being followed
by a guard, all I could hear was a lot of yelling and screaming. Once the pod doors opened, I could hear every inmate
yelling out the top of his lungs. I was still having these heart-
related issues and this only intensified everything. The guard
yells from the control tower over the intercom, "Leary, lock
down now. Go to your cell now."

The screaming and yelling went on tell very early into the
next morning, and I would get no rest. The pod was under
lock down for a riot that had just taken place. It was the
Mexicans against the Blacks. We were locked down for nearly
a week and the yelling and screaming nightly didn't stop.

The guards were rotating inmates in and out once this was
done. The doors were raked open. There was still a lot of ten-
sion in the air. So I then got with one of the White leaders
and one of the Mexican leaders and tried to work out a peace
treaty. I would come to know Larry, who I would become
good friends with once released from prison.

Larry was someone who was looking at a life sentence.
He had so many charges, he was already somewhere around
fifty. The state of Arizona was trying to kill him by stacking so many drug charges on him that it would be impossible for him to complete the time that these charges carried.
They had investigated Larry for nearly eight years and probably spent hundreds of thousands of dollars investigating
him. Eventually, these same cops would have to drop a good
part of their case because, some of their very own law
enforcement personnel had broken the law in his case by
listening to unauthorized telephone conversations. They
were actually listening to conversations that had nothing to

do with drugs. These cops screwed up so bad that the case had to be sealed by Superior Court Judge Dolton. Larry, in my opinion, was a very smart man. Sometimes being to smart could get you in trouble. Larry was also a former drug dealer, who was in prison for manufacturing meth. Larry had made millions from this side job of his. During the time he had been doing in the county jail, he started practicing law. He was the jailhouse lawyer for our pod. He would often joke around, saying that he could help every one else but, he couldn't help himself. The next morning, I would get my first court hearing.

The Judge would read out the new charges. "David Leary, you are being charged with the sale of a controlled substance, cocaine, a Class 2 Felony. How do you plead?"

"Not guilty, your honor," was my response. A potential trial date was set. Upon returning to my cell, I just couldn't believe what was taking place. I only had one year to go in prison, and before I could do the final year on the agreement I have with the State, they rearrested me. It was at this point that my heart begun to beat irregularly again. I had to be taken to the jailhouse hospital, and then later I had to transfer to Maricopa County Hospital. I was really scared all over again. At this point in my life, I really and truly didn't think I would see the streets again.

I began to wonder how much could I take. I already had a mild stroke, now I'm having heart problems. And to top it all off, I was being charged with an old-new crime. This made me pick up my Bible and read. All jokes aside, I thought I was going to die. I believed at this time that because, of the life that I have lived, I had no favors coming from God. But somehow, some way, I knew I needed to establish some kind of link with him. I begin to pray a lot, I was scared out of my mind.

Upon completing a heart test at the county hospital, I was returned to the county jail. This time, I had a heart monitoring devise strapped around my chest that I also had to sleep with. What I was going through with my heart didn't negate the conditions of the county jail. There were people being transferred in and out of the pod. So this shit kept going constantly.

There were fights almost daily and the thought of another riot jumping off was always present and an immediate reality. In my mind I kept wondering, *How much can I take?* I never knew that the God my mother prayed to was also the same God that was trying to get my attention. I thought I was dying, so I was also trying to get his. Larry was my angel, unbeknownst to me; Larry had begun to consult with me daily about my case. Just consulting with Larry on a daily basis made my heart feel better.

If the State of Arizona had gotten their way, I would have been looking at somewhere around 30 years. This alone had created unneeded stress for me. I tried calling the lawyer that had represented me five years ago. This is the same guy who would leave me in the courtroom without saying goodbye. He refused to help me because I didn't have any money. What could I expect? He seemed like a piece of shit from the beginning. He left me before the judge hit the gavel down. I should have known he wouldn't help me. I couldn't find any one who would loan me money to hire a lawyer. I shouldn't have been surprised. The life I had lived wasn't a good one; I still had more dues to pay.

Then Larry began to read my case and informed me that he could help me. He put together a writ of *habeas corpus.*

This basically says that they either had to prosecute me now or let me go. The State of Arizona had waited 8 years to unseal this indictment. By being a little too smart, they exceeded the time limits of a Class 2 Felony which was 7 years, so ultimately the State had to drop the charges with prejudice—meaning that it could never be brought up again. Within two weeks, I was heading back home, back to Fort Grant Prison. I had begun to call prison home because, five long years had gone by while I had been locked up. Besides, I couldn't go anywhere else. Only one year to go. What else could go wrong? I figured I could just glide right through it. I had never been so wrong. This is prison; the shit just doesn't stop here. It seemed that they had finally Institutionalized me. A good example would be two inmates fighting over a 50-cent-per-hour job. A term meaning, basically, being okay with how the system treats you.

Back to Fort Grant Prison, Back to Reality

I had got back to my same pod that night around 8:30 pm. I remember lying in my bed that evening, talking to this white guy about the ordeal I just had undergone when, four guys with hoods on their faces entered the dorm. I knew something serious was about to take place—this was the Hit Squad. To my surprise, they jumped on the guy I was just talking to. They kicked and beat him senselessly. I could hear each punch and kick land to his face and body. They continued to beat on him. I wanted to stop this, but I could not interfere. The quiet rule in prison is that you don't interfere with another race's business.

This was something that could easily trigger another riot. I felt helpless as I sat there and watched the Hit Squad ferociously beat this guy. For a moment, I thought they would kill him. It really bothered me that, I could do nothing to help him. Even if I could have tried to stop it, I would have been no match for 4 guys, especially with my heart condition. So many emotions went on inside my mind as they continued to beat on him. It lasted approximately fifteen minutes, but it seemed longer to me.

As they left the dorm, one of the guys from the Hit Squad yelled out, "Bitch, you better be in the hole by morning, or you will surely die!" The guy I had been talking to just laid there, bleeding. As soon as the Hit Squad left, I yelled to someone, "Get help!"

I found out in the morning that this guy's ex-girlfriend wrote a letter to one of the white leaders on the yard saying that this guy sexually molested her daughter. That's why these four guys assaulted him in the manner that they did. It was brutal. Even after being in prison for years, this is something that I just couldn't get used to.

I never saw that guy again, nor was I able to see the guys who jumped him. To be honest, I don't know if this guy made it out of the hospital. I found out later that the guy had never done anything to this woman's kid; she just wanted to get back at him for leaving her. The Hit Squad nearly killed this guy without first trying to find out if her accusations were really true. That's just one of the many really messed up things about prison. Some of the leaders who run the place aren't necessarily the brightest.

After everything that I had faced in prison, I started to wonder if God would allow me the opportunity to, see the out side of the prison walls again. I had around nine months to go.

I had started to go to church twice a week. I knew it was time to make a genuine change in my life. I didn't realize it at the time, but the God that my mother always reminded me about was indeed watching over me. I was a hard nut to crack; I had to suffer like this in order to see the light. I had became a regular in the prison church, despite the criticism from other inmates. I didn't care what they said. I needed to try and fix me and the Lord God said, "Come as you are." So I went as I was; a disgrace to my family, a menace to society, and a loser in every sense of the word.

As was explained to me back then, God wanted the worst of the worst and surely I fit into that category. I had also started taking classes in college where I would earn a Computer Literacy Certificate. At this point in my life, I was tired of being a nobody. Most importantly I had made a promise to God and I truly did not want to go back to using and selling Cocaine. However, I knew myself. I was still addicted to the lifestyle.

I was just months away from going home and reality was setting in again. I was afraid of the unknown. I was afraid of what could happen if I went back to using and selling once I got out. I was afraid of myself. Whenever I got a chance to use the phone, I would call my mom, who would say, "Son, I'm praying for you." This always brought me comfort. In prison; however, comfort is a temporary thing. After all, it was a breeding ground for misery and it wanted company.

Three Months To Go on the Six-Year Bid and Trouble was Brewing Again. Here, It Just Doesn't End.

Just three months to go and I would experience another night that I would never forget; a night that would send shock waves of fear all over my body. I was awoken at somewhere around 8:30 pm that night by someone saying, "Big D, wake up."

I remember looking up at another inmate. "You'd better get dressed and meet us outside," he said. "We're about to have another riot. Got to get my knife." Just as soon as I stepped out the door, the sirens went off and the cops ran to the Yard Office, where they locked the doors. They, too, were afraid. The guards were yelling on the intercom saying, "All inmates, lock down now! Lock down!" They repeated these orders every two minutes, but no one was listening.

The first thing that went through my mind was, "Damn, not this, not right now."

Once I had thrown my clothes on and walked out the doors, I could see the Mexicans had gathered with the illegal Mexicans. They took up an entire side of the block and were passing knives to each other. They didn't look happy at all.

We stood on the other side of the block and I sized up our army. We were only 50 souls strong and we didn't even take up a quarter of the block. It didn't take me long to figure out what the out come of this would be.

There were about 350 of them, according to my estimate, and they didn't look like they cared about the orders being shouted over the intercom. The sirens kept going off with the shouting of the guards from the Yard Office. "Inmates lock down now! Inmates lock down now!"

We were about to get our asses stomped, if not killed. For the second time in my stay here, fear was in my heart. There is no way we could have stood up to them; there were just too many. Anybody who could believe differently would have to be a fool. I remember the guy who woke me up saying, "What are we going to do, Big D?"

All I could think was, *I'm going home in less than three months.* I yelled out to him, "We are going into immediate negotiations." I was thinking, *I'm so tired of this crazy shit, I want to go home, it just never stops.*

Nevertheless, this has to be dealt with now, or going home would just be a want. This was some real shit that had to be dealt with right away. I remember, going up to the Mexican leader with a few more guys, wondering how we could bring an end to this crisis. They wanted one of the guys in our race beat down and we happily granted the offer. Just as quickly as it had begun, it was over. Eventually, everyone locked down that night before the National Guard was called in.

The very next day, the guy that started this mess, was put into protective custody, along with all that tough stuff he used to preach—he was always running around talking that high-powered shit. Before he went there, he got a beating, one he rightfully deserved. I did not participate in the beating because, I was two months shy of going home, but there were more than enough guys willing to do it. This dude could have gotten a lot of us killed or hurt very badly. I couldn't help but think what could have happened if I was still asleep and the riot had taken place. One can only wonder what the outcome might have been.

Often new inmates come to the yard and think that because of their size, they don't have to follow the rules. No matter how big you are, when you've got ten people coming to get your ass, trust me when I say they will get it. This guy thought he was real tough. Once they got on his ass, he quickly ran to get protection. All that tough stuff was out the window.

November 13, 1996
I'm Going Home

I was scared as hell. I didn't know what was to become of me once I was released, or if I was even going to be released at all. I had made up my mind that morning, not to become excited until, I actually made it out the front gate. After what I had experienced, I didn't have faith in the prison system. I knew one thing for sure, the odds were against me. I was supposed to be going home that morning and so many thoughts were going through my mind. I couldn't leave prison without praying one more time, so I got on my knees. I remember falling to my knees that morning and praying to God, saying, "Please, don't let me return to the lifestyle that I was used to." I truly didn't want to go back to selling drugs. I begged the Lord, "Please help me," as I continued to pray.

My mother taught me to believe that there is a God. At this point in my life, I felt that I didn't deserve to still be standing. I knew, however, that I had a purpose in life; I just didn't know what it was. When my purpose was revealed to me, death, mental anguish and extreme pain came with it.

I remember being in a class called Personal Financial Planning at the Cimarron Unit and the teacher was asking everyone in class what were they going to do with their lives. When he got around to me, I stood up and said, "I know I'm going to be somebody." I just didn't know who or what. One day, out of the blue, this purpose would be revealed to me. I didn't know if my God was listening, but he was, indeed.

Anyone that knows the Lord God knows the quote, "he may not come when you want him, but he is always right on time."

They say in prison that the real test comes when you are released. I would be tested beyond anything that I could have ever have believed. Life as I knew it would change forever again, but this time, the change would be forever and ever.

CHAPTER 10

The Unforeseen Reality:

Death, Destruction and Salvation

Three months out of prison and it's on. Everything that I had promised God I wouldn't do, I was doing—except for actually using the drugs. Once again, I had lost all touch with reality. While knowing that if they caught me selling these drugs, I would be sent to prison for a good part of my life and no one, including my family, would choose to remember me or my life. Once again, I had lied to God and this is not good by any standard.

I started working, doing some home improvement and selling drugs on the side. Everything that I had planned to do while I was in prison was out the window. Getting the right drug connection was priority. I was selling weed and cocaine daily. My nephew and I had become a team in the drug business. Once again, I had allowed my morals to be defeated. Once again, I had disrespected my family values and worse, I had let my God down by not keeping my promise and going back to selling cocaine.

I'm not proud of what I did. In a sense, I had signed up and was working for Satan's Army. My mom had raised me to be a child of God.

I had worked my way up from a forty rock to a kilo g. I was the big dope man again. I was riding around in new cars and not worrying about what I was going to eat for dinner.

Although, thinking alone in quiet moments, I was ashamed of what a messed-up person I had become again. I had allowed this drug to get the best of me again. Sometimes, while still selling Cocaine, something would come over me and I would immediately fall to my knees and start praying and asking forgiveness. I hadn't realized it, but the fight between Good and Evil had begun.

Once off my knees, my cell phone would ring and I would then go and make that sale. I tearfully asked the Lord to help me out of that mess on many occasions. The people I sold drugs to praised me for having the best dope; they gave me high respect. They never wanted me to run out and I tried my best not to run out. However, at home alone, I actually felt like shit, quietly saying to myself, "This is not really what I'm supposed to be doing." It appeared the Beast was back in control.

Unbeknownst to me, I was already receiving the mercy that I was begging for in my prayers.

The Cops, Got Me Jacked on the Freeway. He Smells Dope in the Car and I'm in Handcuffs Once Again

Six months out of prison and there was a drug drought in Phoenix; nobody I knew had any. Nearly no one could find drugs, so with my quick thinking, I figured if I can be the first to come back with some dope, I can get all the money, never taking into account the possibility of something going wrong—like getting pulled over on I-17 in Tucson while driving with my ex-girlfriend, Dawanna and the cop getting his hands on the drugs.

It was the K-9 unit. The cop's first words to me were, "License and registration." He then asked me why I was swerving in traffic. I told him I wasn't. He went back to the car.

Dawanna and I were scared because, the cocaine and weed were in her purse and my fingerprints were on the bags. Worse yet, you could see and smell the drugs, without picking up the purse—there was so much in there, we couldn't close it. As I looked in the rearview mirror and saw that the cop was running my license plate, I realized that going back to prison had suddenly become a very real possibility for my near future.

All I could think of at the time was, *I'm going back to prison. Damn, how can this be actually happening? I've only been out six months.*

I was hoping that I would wake up from what I wished was a real bad dream, but I was already up. As I sat in the car, visibly shaking, the cop approached the car again.

"Why do I smell weed in the car?" he asked.

I responded, "There isn't any weed smell in here."

He ordered me out the car and said, "Mr. Leary, you have a warrant for your arrest." He placed me into the handcuffs and then told Dawanna to get out of the car and stand over to her right. He then shoved my head down, guiding me into the front of the patrol car—the police dog was in the back.

The cop then grabbed the dog from the back seat and walked him around my car. The dog indicated that there were drugs in the car. The cop then locked the dog into the back seat of the patrol car again and did a visual inspection himself. He found Dawanna's purse and the drugs inside.

The first thing I said, still handcuffed in the front seat of the car, was, "Shit, I'm going back to prison."

I could see the cop with the purse in his hands, looking at the dope. To be honest, he didn't have to look because, he could smell it. It reeked of weed and cocaine.

Divine Intervention

Then something happened that I had never witnessed before, or even heard about, in all my years of selling drugs. As I sat there watching, the cop placed the purse back into the front seat of my car. He then came back to his patrol car and took the handcuffs off of me.

"Mr. Leary," he said, "next time, don't be swerving. Have a nice day."

We had two ounces of powder cocaine and a quarter-pound of some very potent marijuana. That kind of shit just doesn't happen. I started off that day with a few stiff drinks and smoked at least three joints before jumping on the freeway. After that incident, I wasn't high any more. Dawanna and I were both shaking when we jumped back into the the car. The drugs were still in her purse. My eyes are naturally big, but were even bigger as I put the keys in the ignition.

"Should we throw the dope out on the freeway?" I asked Dawanna. "Are they going to jack us again up the freeway?" We drove slowly and quietly back to Phoenix, never returning to buy drugs in Tucson. I had witnessed a lot of things in my many years of criminal activity, but never this.

It defored all logic and reasoning. There's no doubt in my mind, the Lord intervened. My true purpose in life had yet to be revealed.

I didn't realize it at this point, but years later I would have another day in court. I was, indeed, destined to go to court again for new charges, but this time, they were charges I would be *pressing* and not *facing*.

When God is blessing us who believe in Him, we often can't see it until it is actually manifested onto us. Exactly one month later, God would pour more of his spirit and blessings upon me. I would meet a woman who would later become my wife.

As usual, I was trying to get my money. I wasn't about to let anyone get in the way of this. I had become Satan's soldier and once again he was my commander. The only thing that worried me was the fear of running out of drugs. I depended on Satan, in a sense because, I depended on his product: cocaine. I wasn't concerned about what could happen to me if I was caught up again. I rode around in my car with this drug constantly, with no restrictions.

All of a sudden, the nightmares started again. I would go to sleep and have visions of myself being locked back in prison. I could hear the sound of keys dangling off a guard's belt and the loud rattling as the guards opened and shut prison doors during body counts. I could see the blinding light of a flashlight in my face, late into the night. I twisted and turned in my sleep every night. These dreams seemed so real that often I would wake up soaking wet from sweating, my heart pounding rapidly in my chest.

I had these dreams almost every night when I was in the dope game. They just wouldn't go away and each time they came, they would appear to be stronger in vision and seem closer to reality.

I was having visions of being locked up again. As I sold drugs, the visions would reappear often and regularly. Once again, the Lord God was seeking my attention, but I wasn't listening. In time, the Lord would seek my total undivided attention and he would surely get it.

Dealing Kilo's of Dope on the West Side of Town: Stacking My Ends

I met up with Jamal, an old acquaintance from back in the days when I was Greedy D. We worked together in the drug business back in the day. I was happy to see him again and he was happier to see me. He told me that he had heard that

I had the good stuff and he wanted in. He told me that he had permission to open up shop on the West Side from one of the main Crips, whom we both knew. He then invited me to his place of business on 13th Avenue and Buckeye and showed me the amount of money that was coming through his shop. Jamal and I hit it off right away. I was his supplier, I promised him that I would never let him run out and he promised me that he would always have my money. Unfotunately, neither one of us would live up to this commitment.

Our bond had grown and we both were making a lot of money. One of the things I liked about Jamal was that he was always respectful, especially when picking up large sums of

money. I had grown to be a little weary of going to the West
Side to pick up my money however, but Jamal was getting
it quickly and sometimes couldn't leave the Rock House. I
would then have to stop what I was doing and make sure the
business kept going. Sometimes, he kind of scared me with
how much he was bringing and how quickly it was coming.
When I would show up to pick up my money at his estab-
lishment, I would ask him, "How are things going?"

He would then show me a big pile of money, smile and
say, "Everything is going just fine, Mr. Dave. I'm doing a full
court press."

I'd explain to him that the undercover police officers were
circling the block. He would then say, "Don't worry about
them. I've got everything under control." He then told me to
"just keep the dope coming."

The fact of the matter is, he didn't have anything under
control; it was all in his mind. Jamal made more money than
me; he also took more of a risk.

He was on the front lines in the drug business. He also
received all the spoils and benefits for taking that type of risk.
Almost every time I went to the Rock House, he had girls
hanging out who would do anything at his command. Jamal
had started making more money than he had ever seen
before. He started wearing robes and sweat suits almost every
day. I used to call him the black Hugh Heffner. He had
become obvious about selling dope at his house.

He began to let some transactions go on outside of the
Rock House. This was the start of his downfall and mine. He
brought a BMW and put some nice rims on it. Every day,
he would have anywhere from five to fifteen people outside
his door. Some were out there, just waiting to get another hit.
Jamal was a hell of a nice guy, but if you shorted his money,
you would see the other side that wasn't nice at all. He was

also a gangster, and a big pimp from way back. That was the only type of guy who could open up business on 13th Ave and Buckeye and get paid. You had to be tough over there to get paid because, the stress factor was always high. You could get killed at any time. He respected me to the utmost because I was even more treacherous then him.

I had become concerned; by the way Jamal was running the business. I told him that this operation wouldn't last and that police was always parked somewhere that they could get a direct view of his door. Once again, he reassured me by saying, "Everything is just fine, Mr. Dave."

I then said to him, "All right, but remember our agreement?"

From then on, whenever I needed to drop off his sack or pick up some money, I would dress up like a smoker, park my car blocks away and walk to the Rock House. I wouldn't wear jewelry or anything that would make me stand out. In the picture on page 208, I was out checking one of my traps at about 4:00 in the morning. I was real serious at this point about collecting my money. I would always make my runs, dropping off my sacks around this time because, there were fewer police officers on the streets and less traffic.

Six Months Later . . .

I stopped going to the Rock House altogether. The police had started sending informants to Jamal. By this time, however, they could never make a buy. My man had gotten a little sloppy with the way he was running the business. Soon the inevitable happened; the police had set up surveillance at all entrances to the Rock House one day, waiting on Jamal to go to his spot. I had just given him a kilo the day before.

When Jamal entered the Avenues, the police jacked him. He had plenty of drugs on him. After all, I had just re-supplied him the day before. Jamal later went to court and said that the drugs were all his. He had realized that this was something he had created and something that he had to live with. He accepted that fact and the time that came with it: four and a half years. He handled it like a man and I respect him for that. There was a time that I had to make that same decision.

Divine Intervention #2

I found out the next morning that my dog had got jacked by the real jackers yesterday: the Police Department. By this time, Perry and I had been working together and we just lost all the money because, we were giving Jamal his supply on credit. To make matters even worse, some how the very next day, I found myself on the West Side with three ounces of dope on my person. I knew this was a no-no, especially after my boy had been taken down on this same side of town, just two days prior. I was with my boy, Eagle, and he was driving his car with his daughter in the back seat.

Before we even got to the West Side, I gave him instructions on what to do if the police came up behind us. By this time, the West Side was hot. If you were black and you didn't look like you belonged over there, even if you were just driving through, you were fixing to get shook down. Your rights had nothing to do with it. The very next thing we knew, a cop car was approaching us. I told my dog, "Don't forget, I got three ounces of rock cocaine on me, man."

Eagle said, "I got this."

As soon as the cop car passed us, it made a U-turn. I told Eagle to pull over, not to let him put on his lights, to let me out the car. This dude once again told me, "I got this."

The fact of the matter was, he didn't have anything. Eagle is a former gang member—all tattooed up. As a matter of fact, we were in his old 'hood, Boot Hill, 13th Ave. It was not a good situation to be in.

The cops hit us with the lights. By the time we pulled over, two more cars pulled up. They ordered us both out of the car. I knew when all the police cars pulled up, it was officially on. They told us we had a cracked windshield, but I knew why they had really pulled us over and it had nothing to do with the windshield. Once again, going back to prison was an immediate possibility. They had just gotten Jamal two days beforehand. Now, it seemed, it was my turn.

First, they asked for identification from both of us. Six Cops surrounded us, asking all kinds of questions about what we were doing over here, while another Cop was, running our IDs. As soon as he had the information he was looking for, they had Eagle out of his shirt and had his pants open, where they could see his private parts. I kept thinking, This can't be really happening, hoping it was a bad dream. The thought of this being a dream would be shattered, once the cops started to ask me questions.

At this point, I started to quiver in my boots. I was watching them look at Eagle and his private parts, saying to myself, *This is it. Why didn't I stop selling dope, after the Tucson incident?*

I was in a daze when the cop yelled at me to take off my shoes. Slowly I grabbed each one and handed them to the cops. One of them said to me, "Leary you ever been arrested before?"

I said, "Yeah."

"For what?" he asked.

I said, "For everything."

There was no reason to lie now. I realized—as he gave me orders to remove my socks, lift up my arms and spread my legs—that I was busted.

As I looked down, I could see the bulge from the three ounces of rock cocaine in my pants. Once the cop looked in my pants, like they were doing to Eagle, or patted me down, he would find the drugs for sure.

The cops then ordered me to turn around so they could search me. One of them ran both hands up my pants and around my waist. When he yelled for me to stand against the car and don't move, I thought for sure that he felt the drugs. As I stood there visibly shaking, I had to think fast. I had to calm down first; I didn't really know what to think at that moment.

After standing there against the car, surrounded by cops and looking down at the bulge in my pants, I thought to myself, *they said that they pulled us over for a cracked windshield.* So after standing there for about fifteen minutes, I said, "Hey man, this is a whole lot, for just a cracked windshield."

The more I talked to them and pointed out the wrong that was taking place, the calmer I felt. As I said, the Cops were searching the car from top to bottom. They wanted the drugs, I had them on me. They even looked into Eagle's little girl's diaper, searching for the drugs. After about 30 minutes of humiliation, they let us both go.

I was very upset with my friend because, he didn't follow my instructions to the T and I was concerned about what had just taken place. I was even more upset with myself for putting my freedom in someone else's hands. I knew that after that, I wouldn't have any more chances to play with. The Lord had gotten me out of my mess again, no doubt about it. I should have gone back to prison, but once again the Lord had shown favor. There was no doubt in my mind that someone greater than I had intervened in the matter. However, this wasn't enough to kill the desire I had to sell drugs. I kept selling my drugs daily with no restrictions. However, the dreams continued and the visions of going back to prison was closer to becoming a reality.

My conscience started eating at me. Most drug dealers don't have one, but I did.

I also thought about what my purpose in life was. I knew that narrowly escaping getting arrested on the West Side was my last chance and that the next incident, I would surely return to prison because, I wasn't hearing the Lord God speaking to me. It was like I couldn't stop selling the drugs.

The dreams continued and all of a sudden the thoughts of going back to prison were starting to play out in my mind constantly. I would often be at home, sitting on the couch, imagining the door being kicked open and the police running inside. I would take my drugs from one hiding place in the house to the next. I couldn't get this thought out of my mind; from sun up to sun down, the thoughts of the Police invading my privacy again haunted me.

Often while I was at home, a car would drive down the street and in my mind, it was the cops. Nothing could stop the dreams and the visions of the police coming. The nightmares became a regular occurance. Paranoia started setting in again.

Then something happened that had never happened before: I felt the strong desire to go to church and to keep going. That's when my world started to change. This was different than all the times before. In a way, I can't explain it; I had been to church before.

I will never forget the words of my mother, who always said, "Son if you got problems, give it to God. He will fight your battles."

However, the drug selling wouldn't stop. I began to pray more and often after praying, I would end up in tears, begging the Lord for mercy, something that I knew that I didn't deserve. I knew selling cocaine was wrong, but after selling drugs since 1977, which was actually when I first had gotten weed to sell, I was addicted to selling them. I was addicted to the power it gave me, to the money that it made me. And now, these drugs were more powerful than ever before.

No matter what criminal activity I was involved in, I had never stopped asking God to intervene in the matter. I knew at this point, I was insane once again. Why else would I get out of prison and go immediately back to selling drugs, knowing how much time that they would give me if I got caught?

I started attending church and God started working on me. Often I would see some of the people that I was selling dope to there. I would often pray to God about the things I was doing that I knew were wrong, while picking up the dope sack after church services to make a sale, which was messing with my conscience. I had a conscience because of the values that my mother instilled in me as a kid, but I had lost my soul. By selling cocaine, I had pledged my allegiance to Satan, to the Beast. I sometimes went to church with rock cocaine on me, just in case I needed to make a quick sale afterwards or, depending on the amount of the sale, I would go during.

I was starting to feel that Satan was in me and at times, he was calling all the shots. I felt hypocritical as the services went on, especially because in some occasions I sat in the church with cocaine on me. Even so, I had come to the Lord just as I was. The more I showed up at church, the more I realized that I had to make a choice and the more my conscience would bother me. As my mother always said, "Son, you can't serve two Masters."

The Beast simply didn't want to let go of me. After all, he had controlled me for over 24 years.

While praying, I would ask God to help me to overcome this thing. I didn't want to lose my family and die in prison. I knew that if I went back to prison, I would die there and my soul would die there, too. If I went back to prison, the Beast would have had the glory.

Sometimes, during church services, I would cry out to him for help, and I was, indeed, sincere. Immediately after church, I would go make a drug sale. The thought of the police coming wouldn't stop and neither would the dreams. I became emotionally unstable and paranoid. My inner mind spoke to me more. There was no doubt in my mind that the fight between Good and Evil was in motion and nearly at its peak. I found myself praying on my knees, saying, "God help me." My soul was at war. Good and Evil was at war inside of me.

I would go to church and it was like everybody knew I was a drug dealer and it seemed the preacher was always speaking directly to me. The fact of the matter was, no one other than the people who I sold to knew I was a dope dealer; this was just part of the emotional struggle that was going on inside my mind. As a matter of fact, I had seen one of the girls that I used to sell drugs to in church with her parents.

One of the reasons I knew these were her parents was because, I had recently been invited over to her house and she put me on the spot with her parents saying that, she owed me $200 for a drug deal and that I was her drug connection. At this point in my life, I was drinking alcohol almost every day. This fight between Good and Evil would not stop as long as I picked up the dope sack. Now the struggle was getting harder to deal with inside my mind because every time I would make a sale, I would think about church and what the preacher was saying. The fight between Good and Evil would increase.

The thought of the police coming did not stop. In many cases, I was an emotional wreck and I knew that someone greater than I was the only one who could help me. At this point, almost every day I was saying a prayer and I was getting less sleep at night. Almost every other dream was of the guards in prison doing head count, flashing the light in my face. This is what would wake me up out of the dreams. In all cases, I would be sweating profusely and my heart would beat violently. I would then wonder about selling drugs and why I kept doing this. I'd think about church and what the preacher said. Somehow, I knew that something would have to give. My mother was right when she said I couldn't serve two Masters. This would go on for some time when all of a sudden, my purpose in life was revealed to me.

No matter what you do in life, if you forget about God, he has a way of getting your undivided attention. My Lord God started speaking to my heart and he shook up my entire life. It was at this point that I knew that selling hard drugs would be over for me, forever.

The Lord God's Blessings
are Manifested unto Me

July 4th, 2001: Our mother, Katherine Johnson, died on this day. Death, for her, was her sole comfort. I was the protector of her dignity, which she rightfully deserved and could not be denied. After my mother died, my transformation was complete. Katherine Johnson, my mother, did not have an easy life nor did she have an easy crossover to the afterlife. All my mother only knew in life was suffering, suffering beyond anyone's imagination. But through the power of God, she would have justice.

My Lord God has freed me from cocaine's grip, the Devil's lure and the Beast's power. Now I know why I had to go through everything that was discussed in this book. God actually wants the worst of the worst. My life repre-

sented just that. The Lord God has proven—not that he had to—that if he can change me, everyone else should be easy. He has changed me. There's nothing like the feeling of being able to walk out my door and not be afraid of being arrested, or even worse, killed, for my dope sack. I had been bound for so many years and now I'm free, all glory to God, my Creator.

At one time in my life, this just wasn't a possibility, at least, not that I could see. *Thank you Jesus.* I've been with the same woman for over ten years. There is a life worth living. Most addicts can only see what's in front of them, but with faith the size of a mustard seed, anyone can have their soul back. I've been to hell and God alone has showed mercy in my life and brought me back. He can do the same thing for you because, he can do anything. He has proven that in my case. He alone deserves the praise; he alone is worthy.

In her lifetime, my mother couldn't give us what she wanted us to have. No one could have ever imagined that this same poor soul would change the lives of many, upon her death. When Katherine Johnson was alive, she may have thought her life was insignificant—she never owned any real property and she never owned or drove a car. Even she could not have known that her death would change many lives in the great state of Arizona, starting with her son and grandson and spreading to those she never had a chance to meet.

God has restored my life back to normalcy. He has brought me back from the dead and I say this because the Beast was literally trying to destroy my soul. I finally have my soul back. Because of what has taken place in my life, I'm finally living the life for which my mother always prayed for me, one in which God would be the leader of our home. She never gave up on me, as she had promised. In a sense, I didn't give up on her either. I'm so glad God has restored my life and has given me purpose. Now I feel whole. For once in my life, I truly feel like a winner.

May the Lord God, forever merciful and true, continue to use me to reach out to thousands of souls who are suffering at this very minute from these menaces to society, with this message of hope and with this book.

"God can do anything, son," my mother always said. "Only the Father is the perfect one and he alone has the power to do anything."

She also said that, "When we, as human beings, try to fix things, that's when it all gets messed up." She then went on to say, "Son, give it to God, let him fight your battles."

My mother had a sign on her window that read, "The Lord So Loved the World that He Gave His Only Begotten Son. And Who Shall Ever Believe in Him, Shall Not Parish, But They Shall Have Everlasting Life." She believed in Jesus as her Savior, so this means I will see her again. I'm living proof that God can do anything.

I'm finally the son, you've always wanted me to be, Mother. Now you can be proud of me and my nephew, your other son. Now you can have peace knowing that your teachings were not in vain. I love you, Mother. And I'm going to do what you told me to do and that's to be a man and always look after my brother, my nephew.

When I took this picture, I didn't realize that this would be our final picture together. I could not have known as a kid that I would be the one chosen to tell this story. I could not have known that one day I would be chosen by my God to be her sole protector. It's strange the way life really is. Especially growing up as a child, you never know what hand you are going to be dealt. I remember my mother always praying to God, she didn't give up and in a sense, God was all she had. In our minds, all we had was our mother. For sure, God had all of us.

My life has changed dramatically. We now live a normal life. I also make it a habit to talk to people who are bound by these hard drugs with a message of hope.

Anyone can change. I've been married for seven years with four children. I don't know what the future has in store for us, but I do know I will never ever do the work of the Beast, Satan, again.

May the Lord God's will be done in my life.

Thanks again for allowing me to share this true and unique story of change.

May Arizona never forget the name of Katherine Johnson.

I have learned in my life to never ever question God.

Author's Note

The words "nigger" and "nigga" were used
in this book to describe actual events. It is this
author's belief that these words are degrading
and derogatory towards black people in general
and these words were used with reluctance.

Destroyer of Souls:

An extraordinary look at change

Few people can go to the other side and come back normal. Some never come back at all and the final reward is death and destruction, not just to the body, but also to the soul. Beware the lure of drugs are huge profits, that dollar bill.

Satan is the true destroyer of souls. He is a liar. When you've struggled all your life and it seems like there's no way out, it could be real easy to lose your soul. It's tempting when you are walking and you have been doing it for a long time and people drive by you in Cadillac trucks with the big rims and you have been working so hard, just trying to save enough for a car.

You may not have enough education to land that job that can help you to excel and it would seem that there is no end in sight. It could be easy to lose your soul. When you are high-rolling, making hundreds of thousands monthly and sometimes daily, it could be easy to lose your soul. It's hard when you are staring at the potential of making hundreds of thousands of dollars and in some cases, millions.

This is how Satan steals your soul and this is how he stole mine. For years while in the dope game, I received a lot of praise and it made me feel like a king. When I was around my closest friends, I would often tell them that I felt like shit, I felt like a real loser. Once again, I sold my soul to Satan. Once again, I was working for the Beast. Even when it appeared that I was winning, I was actually losing, as I drove my brand-new cars.

Prison and death were lurking behind every drug transaction for me. On the inside, I knew what it was doing to the people, I could see what it was doing to me and in many of the cases, I felt powerless to stop what I was doing because, I was addicted to the power that selling hard drugs had given me. I was like a king to the people I sold drugs too. I knew it would take someone greater than myself to save me because, I was just too far gone. Even the threat of going back to prison didn't matter. Because of my hardcore lifestyle and my sexual addiction to these drugs, I was destined to fail. It was also eating at me that, I would sell drugs to a pregnant woman. No one was off limits, not even family members. The Beast was in total control of my soul.

It would appear that I cared about nothing and no one. Often while I was driving around, I would see these women walking around strung out on these drugs. Looking crazy, stinking—most would do anything for the next hit of cocaine and some would actually be talking to themselves. It didn't matter what color they were. What if this was your momma or your daughter? They were someone's momma, someone's daughter. That was the part of the drug business that was turning my stomach; that was the part that was eating at my soul.

My mother had raised me to respect all women. I was committing genocide. For this reason and more, I don't deserve to live on God's green earth. God chose to put purpose in my life and understanding. I'm forever grateful.

If you are struggling in your life with some of these same issues, I know He can do the same thing for you. Don't believe me. Don't believe these stories. Look at all the success stories. Satan is a liar. You, too, can have your soul back. I won't allow the Beast to ever steal my soul again.

For once in my life, I feel like a real winner. God is the only one worthy of this type of change. To be totally honest, I could never see an exit plan from the dope game, that's how sick I was with it. I just knew that one day, it had to end. I just never knew how. I often wondered if it would end with the taking of someone's life, not excluding mine. When God stepped in, he got my total undivided attention.

All Praises to the Lord God, whose mercy is ever-lasting. He alone could have mercy for someone like me, who doesn't deserve to call upon his name.

Life or death, there's nothing in between. You have to make a choice in life. It is said, "Fear only the one who can kill the body and also the soul."